The Language of Creation

Also by Tantra Maat:

An Irish Tale of a Modern Mystic
published 2010

The Language *of* Creation

Your Original Design

Tantra Maat

The Language of Creation
Your Original Design

iUniverse books may be ordered through booksellers or by contacting:

iUniverse
1663 Liberty Drive
Bloomington, IN 47403
www.iuniverse.com
1-800-Authors (1-800-288-4677)

ISBN: 978-1-4917-0708-1 (sc)
ISBN: 978-1-4917-0709-8 (e)

Print information available on the last page.

iUniverse rev. date: 06/17/2016

Table of Contents

To my clients

Without you,
I could not see what I got to see or know what I got to know.

Seeing your beauty and the wonder of your ingenious design
had me fight to discover what would have you remember.

That is why this book is dedicated to you.

"Language is very powerful.
Language does not just describe reality.
Language creates the reality it describes."
Desmond Tutu

Foreword

When I first read about Tantra's Language of Creation Exercises they reminded me of the neurofeedback exercises we used at the Addiction Treatment Center where I worked as a staff psychotherapist. The neurofeedback exercises worked to restore the brain to its pre-addiction chemistry. Tantra Maat's Creation Exercises reconnect your brain to your spirit. They are like a form of spiritual neuropsychology.

After doing the Creation Exercises I was stilled to actually feel myself returning to the call of my spirit. Quietly sinking inward, I was bypassing layers of cultural and emotional conditioning. I felt more 'me'. I felt more connected to my true self and my truest calling.

I noted that this form of 'creating' felt deeper than other forms of visioning I had practiced as it caused me to make the space for my intuition to reveal, to discover. I simply needed to 'wait on myself' and let my responses rise on their own. Soon it became a joyful adventure! Soon I started moving through the exercises with ease and curious anticipation. What might I find next? What else is in there?

The 'Templates' drew me into places inside myself I'd neglected. Each sentence of the Templates took me further into my unconscious, revealing truths about myself I had been missing. Each paragraph helped me create a stronger and stronger field of vibration that would draw my desired outcome. Slowly I began to see the brilliance of the Templates' design. I began to understand what Tantra calls 'depth of field'. I love that these Exercises are based on Quantum Field Theory. I started to understand why her work, with the vastness of her mystical lineage, appealed to me more than so many other contemporary teachers.

Sometimes the Creation Exercises work really fast! A fellow participant in one of Tantra's classes and I both wrote exercises craving what we wanted in our relationships with our significant others. Within 4 days both of us had broken up with our current partners! Guess they weren't the right partners! Out with the old, in with the new! Make room for what is the best vibrational match for your spirit.

Thank you Tantra for your powerful contribution to the realm of creating. Thank you for your immeasurable contribution to my life.

These exercises are for everyone, especially those who appreciate depth, multi-dimensionality and the call of the mystical. They will help you bring your desires into form, through the intelligence of your spirit. They will assist you in getting the life you really want to live. These are sacred tools that give you the power to launch into this Age of Ascendance with joy.

Come fly with us!

> Callie Shively, MA, LMFT
> Marriage and Family Therapist
>
> August 28th 2013

Introduction

Imagine a tiger having an insight that he was a tiger without having access to the innate design of what a tiger is.

Then imagine he simply awakened to being a tiger again . . .

Imagine what life might be like if you could simply trigger your own unique and innate design—*your own Original Design*—and suddenly found yourself being awake to:

Being what you came to be

Doing what you came to do

Having what you came to have

What if you simply awakened being YOU again?

Imagine being yourself with your own thoughts, your own knowing, and your own way of being . . .

[pause & breathe]

There is a Language of Creation, within which we all exist, whether a sun, a tiger, or a human being.

The flower opening toward the sun . . . is that language.

The spiritual feeling of being one with God . . . is that language.

The smile on a mother's face when the infant is placed in her arms . . . is that language.

The tears in our eyes when we feel heard or feel seen . . . are that language.

Revelation . . . is that language.

Innate comprehension of what we are . . . is that language.

Over the course of time, we have forgotten.

But now, once again, something is stirring.

Something is Awakening . . .

For almost half a century I have worked with people doing what I, as a psychic and seer, call 'readings', or what are known professionally as consultations. During consultations more happened than just giving out information. When I shared what I was present to, clients recognized what I said as accurate. In fact they too, on some level, had been aware of what was revealed. They just had had no access to it. Then the amazing would occur. Access to what was real for them began to surface out of these readings. As I spoke with them, they experienced a stronger sense of being, stamina for what was before them, and peace of mind. The more they listened to the recordings of these readings, the more access they gained. An awareness of their own unique being began to prevail over the weakness and disorientation of the misinformation that had enculturated them. Their lives and their minds could orient to what they knew. They shifted out of the isolation and unconsciousness of being separated from their true design and began to experience, without their realizing it, the actualizing power of their Original Design. They suddenly began to awaken to who they truly were, like the tiger awakening and remembering what it is to be a tiger.

I began to examine what was present when I did a reading and what happened to people over time. I found that when the person remembered, they could trust their knowing and their lives came back online, their Original Design awakened.

They woke up.

They were empowered and self-actualized. The way I languaged seemed to activate a kind of systemic regeneration. A design of reconnection seemed hidden in where the words were coming from. "What is that?" I wondered. I seemed to be sharing information that activated something forgotten. What if people could get access to remembering without me? If I could get access to their Original Design, then they should be able to access their Original Design also. The recognition of something behind the words and the information that aligned people with their Original Design began a path of discovery for me.

Driven by a deep need for this extraordinary design of a human being to be remembered and awakened, I began to explore what would return people to their own knowing and have their lives actualize and manifest that knowing. My persistent thought was, "What happened to us as a species that had us forget? What is it that has such self-defeating thoughts and perceptions loom so strongly in our existence?" I pursued three questions: "What is a human being actually designed to be?", "What is our Original Design?", and, "What could restore that design in our thinking and in actualizing our lives?"

I saw how handicapped people were when they could not hear themselves or be their own seers. I knew how important it was for people to experience their connection to life without having to use anyone else as an authority. I knew it was essential for people to trust their thoughts and feelings more than anything I would say. I was only there to provide validation for what they already knew and insight into the deeper meaning of what was happening in their lives. Their job was to only take in what resonated for them. I knew it was more powerful to use me as a resource to enhance and strengthen their own self-trust than to use me as a substitute for their own awareness. As a seer, I knew we were moving into times when human beings would need to trust and follow their own knowing, trust their own sight. As a prophetess, I knew the times were coming when each person's self-trust and self-awareness would be the primary principles that shaped new futures for humankind.

However, there is a difference between trying to figure out what we are and actualizing what we are. Trying is quite different from actualizing because in actualizing we are simply being what we came to be. Like the famous words of the Jedi Knight, Yoda, in Star Wars "Do or do not, there is no try".

The information I needed came together at the turn of the century. I created linguistic Templates that, when used to exercise the brain, awakened in each person what they were uniquely designed to be. In that awakening, each person could create their unique contribution to Creation, as Creation.

Each person would think with their own unique and essential Language of Creation.

Your thoughts are not your thoughts.
Your thoughts are what you were born into thinking.

You see we have all ended up with a common problem: something is wrong with the way our minds organize thought. Organizing thought in alignment with what created us is the key. By shifting our thoughts to operate in a particular way opens us up into our Original Design. The Templates I created were clear gateways into shifting how the neural synapses of the brain functioned. When the neural synapses shift into resonance with what created us, realities that are ours to embody, occur.

The exercises and the knowledge in this book will awaken you up into the miraculous design of you. The reality of you is simple: Be yourself. But until recent times, the reality of you has not been accessible.

The true magic of manifestation is simple:

When you no longer have to be what you are not,
What is yours to be,
Yours to have,
Yours to do
is Natural.

It is your destiny now to experience yourself as part of the greater intelligence that created you and discover who you are as a unique and essential aspect of that intelligence. That intelligence is Creation. You are created from that intelligence.

When creation organizes your thoughts, based in your own unique languaging, you discover the *real you,* the *you* that is a unique and essential design to Creation. The Language of Creation is unique to you. You discover your own resonant language that stirs awake frequencies within your cells and your spirit that connects you to your birthright, as a unique and essential embodiment of Creation. The Language of Creation lives in all life. The Language of Creation is where all life, including you, operates and moves as a single unfolding wholeness with essential and unique parts. In this Language of Creation, you shift more and more into the reality of unity, oneness, and wholeness that is stirring within you.

Even if you never fully comprehend what is written in these pages, the result will be the same. I have written this book to take you on a journey. This book is not a normal journey. As you turn each page, as you journey through information, exercises, activations, and altered states, your discovery of you will unfold.

You will discover in unity with your spirit and your flesh, your higher and lower minds, your energy and matter, your alchemy and your biochemistry, what you were designed by Creation to be.

That is the promise of these pages:
To Awaken your Original Design.

[pause & breathe]

Meditation

[READ THROUGH SLOWLY]

[BE AWARE OF YOUR BREATH]

[Breathe in] First there is nothing. Then something occurs.
[Breathe out]

[Breathe in] Something formless begins to quiver and move.
[Let your breath release]

[Breathe in] The Universe is forming . . . through energy,
vibration and sound. [Breathe out]

[Breathe in] Energy is the substance of Creation. [Breathe Out]

[Breathe in] Energy condenses into matter. [Breathe Out]

[Breathe in] Vibration sets the pulse of creation. [Breathe Out]

[Breathe in] Sound resonates into manifestation. [Breathe Out]

[Breathe in] The formless becomes form. [Release your breath]

[Breathe in] Realities begin to form. [Breathe out]

We begin to be created.

1

The Forming of Realities

Two people strolling down the street may look like they are living in the same reality. They are not. One person is lost in thought, trying to figure out what is going on and what to do. The other person may be thinking about what is going on and what to do, but is not trying to figure it out. This person is being present to their connection to life; both life around them and their life within, looking within and without for what connects them to life and has them exist as whole.

The aware person moves as part of the whole, responding more than thinking to what is theirs to do, theirs to be, and theirs to have. The other person is lost between their ears and, at best, has only brief moments of feeling connected to life. They can only react to the cluttered content of their mind.

We may never know why reality can be so different for human beings during these times.

Perhaps we are in a species evolution as we were before, where one type of humanoid moves forward into a new way of existing, as with the Cro-Magnons[1], and another type of humanoid goes out of existence. Maybe some of us are beginning to remember and our connection to life is rising again after having lost that connection through events in our long forgotten past. Maybe others can't remember. Maybe nothing else is happening except we are simply in another moment in time when the human race skirts the edge of destruction and we are learning new ways to exist. Or maybe we will never really know what is happening during these times.

---

[1] Cro-Magnon is a name that has been used to describe the first early modern humans.

The point is, however, that something is indeed happening. And what is happening is affecting the very foundation of what we hold reality to be.

Let's stop for a minute and look at outrageous new understandings about reality.

First: there is not one reality.

Multiple cultures, diverse beliefs, and a quantum number of explanations as to why things are the way they are is evidence that there must be more than one form of reality on this planet. More than one way things can be real.

As some of us move into an expansion of knowing what is occurring during these times, we will recognize that there are many realities. That reality is as diverse as beliefs, that each reality is like a culture that has ways and means that have it exist, and that how each reality comes into existence is completely different from how another reality comes into existence.

Second: Reality is not fixed. It is created.

Our present day realities seem to be created by two very distinctly different designs.

There are realities formed from fear, disconnection, and separation and realities formed from love, connection, and unity. The reality of fear, disconnection, and separation was already an existing reality before we came here. In other words, we were born into the reality of separation which collapsed us in a state of limbo and isolation.

How many people say, "I don't belong here." So even though we were born into a reality of separation we still remember belonging to other realities of connection, and love. Not everyone was born into realities of disconnection. Many of the indigenous tribes of our planet still exist in a reality that connects them to all life and keeps them related to the unity of all things.

Third: There are both individual realities and collective realities.

Each of us came to create our own reality here. Each of us carries an Original Design of reality that we came here to embody and actualize. As we actualize what is real for us we find what fits with that real-ness. Although we can learn to adapt to a reality of disconnection, nothing really fits. Even though we can learn to cope with the reality we were born into, something is always missing. Over the next decade, human beings will actualize their own unique design of reality more and more. When we embody the reality we were designed to exist in, a natural state of connection occurs with others who are actualizing their own unique design of reality and thus realities of unity begin to exist. Although there is no reality that we cannot interact with, we are not designed to participate in all realities. We cannot necessarily survive every reality. The lamb can lie down with the lion but probably should move on when he gets hungry.

Fourth: The construct of our thoughts hold reality in place.

To get access to our reality, we must get access to our thoughts.

This book is not only an introduction to a Language of Creation that gives you access to your real thoughts of your Original Design and the reality within which those thoughts exist, this book is the future reality of unity calling.

We cannot stop the shifting of our existence during these times. There is an exodus of people who are leaving the realities of separation and wandering through the wilderness looking for the realities of unity. A body of humanity is on the verge of restoring the wholeness of their Original Design and birthing the realities that come with those designs.

Life is different for me. The reality of separation I was born into, the reality that kept me from what I was actually designed to be, no longer leaks into the unified experience of living that I am in now. I no longer lose myself in realities that are not part of my reality. What I am part of and I operate as are one and I am constantly maturing as that connection.

Because I am part of the reality I exist in, there is no place to *put* me. I cannot be chopped up, categorized, or labeled. I am the reality I am designed to be—being what is mine to be, doing what is mine to do, and having what is mine to have.

It is the grace of this embodiment that gifted me the opportunity to support and participate with others who are emerging out of realities of separation into realities that carry their original connection with life, the Original Design of their unique reality, formed by the power of Creation itself.

These are exciting times. We are awakening into what we were each originally designed to be, our natural state of being. We have the ability now to impact what damaged our systems of unity, oneness, and wholeness. We can now realize our Original Design.

Let's begin with what happened that had us lose touch with what each of us was originally designed to be.

Trauma & Separation

Many of us once existed as part of a unity-based survival system that thrived on unity not fear. We often speak of remembering a reality beyond the separated, fear-based survival system we exist within today. Our survival once connected us to inspired ways of living, creativity, and being alive.

When we think about it, we cannot feel fragmented if we did not once remember being whole, right? In fact, it is our cells that still remember our being systemically whole and connected to a great living energy of which we were an integral part. Our lives were once mutually beneficial and cooperative with the world around us. We were connected to truths that only exist in a unity-based system. If we didn't experience this way of existing at some point in our cellular memory, we wouldn't suffer for the loss of it in our present reality, a loss that has actually deeply imprinted this reality.

Unfortunately, what we don't remember is what actually happened to cause this trauma. Somewhere back in time, something went wrong . . . terribly wrong. Something happened to us. We got separated from our connection to the world around us and to the great living intelligence of which we were a part. We began to operate in a separated state.

What if we did not fall from grace nor chose separation? As far as I know, there is no evidence of our choosing separation. Now that we have more knowledge available to us of what happened on our physical planet, there is evidence of several severe and terrifying events that left human beings not trusting the Earth they had been born into or their relationship with it. Some of those events were meteors that struck a thriving planet and turned the sky into grey ash for over a hundred years. On other levels there may have been visitations from what we thought were "gods" that placed us in a submissive relationship. Or maybe some of us came here as advanced beings from advanced systems and did not take into account the power of the Earth and her chaotic dualistic design. Perhaps we found we could not overcome the influence of this more primitive setting.

The important thing is not what happened to us but how what happened affected us as a species. Imagine what it must have been like. We, for whatever reason, were suddenly cut off from what gave us our connection to Creation. When that happened, when we were cut off from what gave us life, trauma occurred, and shock followed. The problem was the trauma set in at our cellular level. We have adapted to this trauma by living mostly in fear of life driven by insane worries about our survival instead of being one with Creation.

This is where the miraculous system of our Original Design comes into play. We are highly developed survival-based beings. When the traumas occurred and fear followed, powerful survival mechanisms within us activated and stopped the disconnection from completely destroying us. We had fail-safe mechanisms that saved us from extinction.

How did we survive?

We temporarily shut down.

We became emotionally numb, physically desensitized, and mentally asleep. We became dormant. Not dead . . . just no longer available to the full connection to Creation that we once were capable of. These mechanisms continued to preserve us until conditions for being fully alive were restored. Similar to when a computer malfunctions, the operating system has a 'safety mode' which gives access to only the basic functions preserving the computer until its full function is restored.

Deeply wounded by trauma, our relationship to being alive degraded.

[pause & breathe]

Everything, from the function of our minds to the creation of our cultural norms, was constructed from this traumatized state. We began to think that life was something we had to cope with.

Coping took the place of being alive.

We no longer remembered what had happened.

However, not only did these amazing survival mechanisms protect us from extinction, they also helped us to adapt and subsist in a reality of separation. Trauma-based protective armoring developed that protected us from experiencing the memory of loss. We developed beliefs and actions that held in place our separation from our original connection to ourselves, others, and life. Fear became the primary motivator, not love.

[pause & breathe]

Miraculously, though, buried deep within our DNA were encodings of remembrance. When conditions were right these encodings would activate and we would begin to awaken to the preciousness of our Original Design.

Conditions are finally right. The need to remember is not only because of our emerging consciousness of selfhood, but:

> If we don't remember our Original Design of a trauma-free
> existence, the escalating trauma-based violence sweeping
> our planet will annihilate us.

These DNA encodings are now stirring.

We are now in a time that changes everything. In fact we are in the throes of it! The survival mechanisms that locked us down to safeguard our survival are unlocking. The coping skills we developed to endure that old trauma are now failing. It is time for our operating systems to return to full function and get out of 'safety mode'.

What we bet on, up until now, to get us through life, is no longer sufficient. What we have been told is quickly becoming insufficient and redundant. The inner core of our matter is awakening at such an accelerated rate, our minds and our bodies are being challenged by the unfamiliar. Conditions, both external and internal, that restore our connection to life, are rising as the fear-based fail-safe modes fail. We are being compelled to examine our beliefs about what is going on, finding that what we have believed up until now, does not explain what we are experiencing. Whole new visions of life are pressing up out of our depths, opening us into whole new relationships with ourselves.

We are awakening to the discovery that much of what we have believed, in fact, isn't real.

Awakening is no longer secreted away in unconventional thinking.

Awakening is what is happening.

We just had no idea it would look or feel like it does. We have mistaken awakening for overwhelm, physical exhaustion, mental confusion, emotional anxiety. What we are experiencing, the old systems of understanding cannot sort out. Medical and religious answers no longer explain what is happening.

Our minds and bodies are releasing back into the Language of Creation. Our entire system is actively restoring our Original Design.

We are in the shock of our systems returning to being an integral part of life. New perceptions and applications are now demanded.

After eons of time, we are in a powerful creative process as our Original Design reformats our minds, re-configures our bodies, and reboots our systems.

> We must rediscover ourselves during this cellular
> awakening. Learn about what is occurring. Support each
> other in the shift. Awaken as the new information and
> sensory systems rise within us.

> We are returning to wholeness.

> [pause & breathe]

Language

> "If words were natural rather than cultural,
> we would all speak the same language."
> Ferdinand de Saussure, linguist

In an indigenous language there is nothing that separates the person who speaks that language from the world around them. That kind of language lives in unity with all life, creates the experience of connection with a greater design, and bonds them to others of their tribe.

> "When we realize that language creates reality, we recognize
> the difficulty to accept the fact that it is through,
> and by means of, words that we see and understand
> (or even misunderstand) what we call reality."
> Steven C. Scheer[2] (Hungarian English professor)

---

[2] *Words Matter: Does Language Create Reality?* (n.d.). Retrieved from http://stevencscheers.blogspot.ie/2007/07/does-language-create-reality.html

So if there are two realities, one that separates us from ourselves and one that connects us to ourselves, it follows that the language of these realities either separates us from ourselves or connects us to ourselves. These designs of language either separate us from life or connect us to life. Language gives us access to something or denies us access to something.

> "Although all observers may be confronted by the same
> physical evidence in the form of experiential data and
> although they may be capable of 'externally similar
> acts of observation', 'a person's picture of the Universe',
> or 'view of the world' differs as a function of the particular
> language or languages that person knows." Lee, 1996[3]

We were born into a reality that separates so our language largely formed from our disconnection from the world around us. Perhaps one could even argue that the need for language itself arose from this disconnection because when one is in direct connection, in direct relationship, ultimately there is no need for language, one is simply 'of it', or one with it.

As we have moved further and further away from our connection to the Earth and the Cosmos, our view of our existence has become more and more limited in perspective. What we are left with is the voices in our heads that rattle on in a closed-loop. These voices continuously assess our performance and point out our shortcomings. These voices drone on, keeping us in constant judgment of ourselves, our circumstances, and pretty much everything else 24/7.

For now, let's focus on what could have caused the disconnection.

Language forms from life experience. Some of our language formed when the Earth lost its ability to support us. For instance, when meteorites, over time, collided with the Earth, the fragile innate connection to the Earth our ancestors carried was disrupted and those ancient humans were thrown into turmoil. Other things also happened that formed myths about gods and their displeasure, for example when

---

3   Elgin, S. H. (2000). *The Language Imperative: The Power of Language to Enrich Your Life and Expand Your Mind*. New York: Basic Books.

the moon blotted out the sun during eclipses. The knowledge that would have explained what happened to us during those times was not available then, so Earth events became laced in myth.

Those myths became the basis of reality.

One of the saddest myths about our connection to Creation is found in the myths that gave us our belief in a greater power . . . God, Allah, Jehovah, etc. Much of humanity still holds onto these myths as literal truth. Yet many people now realize that these myths that were created are not true. We were never designed to be separate from what created us. Without understanding what happened, myths got created that we were flawed, that we had somehow, in our innocence, done something atrocious and had fallen from grace. We have even been told that we chose separation.

What did happen is we began to experience ourselves as broken, no longer part of the greater reality we once trusted. God became a perfect being, a feared being, and one that we needed to be perfect for, and allegiant to, to be worthy to be in the presence of. We have spent lifetime after lifetime trying to be perfect to compensate for this deep sense of separation and unworthiness. Now our reality almost completely reinforces that we are flawed, broken, and separate from what created us. It is so sad. It is one of the saddest myths in our present reality.

Can we not see that if God created us, if we are part of God and God is part of us, it doesn't make sense that we would be flawed? Maybe stupid, maybe not fully grown, maybe not fully understanding what we are, but flawed?

No.

And yet even today, many spiritual practices reinforce these myths of separation.

Our myths have been formed by the trauma of being separated from our original connection to Creation and, sadly, our current reality is pervaded by these myths, e.g., religions, wars, etc. So you could say that these myths formed the basis of our reality and thus the basis of our current language—leaving us with a language of separation—which in turn serves to perpetuate the reality of separation.

This is how you think in a language of separation:

1. You find yourself looking for answers in a sea of no answers or conflicting answers. When or if you find the answer or choose the answer you think is best, you still doubt your choice.
2. You can only think you are for something or against something.
3. You think either/or, good or bad, right or wrong, etc.
4. If you think about including something you have to exclude something else.
5. You have to make sure you can explain what you are thinking. You need to understand or be understood.
6. When you think with the present way thought occurs, you can think about something, but thinking about is not the same as thinking with.

In a language of separation, all that you can do is parrot knowledge without having the experience of the knowledge. This occurs mostly in belief where people believe they know what is true without actually having a real experience of it being true.

The present language of separation moves from the past to the future, often referred to as linear thought. Thoughts are often life defeating and internally debasing as we think we have to prove we are of value and prove that we have a right to be here.

Our present language base is object oriented, not connection oriented. Our thoughts further disconnect us from ourselves and each other, excluding more than including, narrowing our life experience. We are left trapped in our thoughts, like a mouse on a treadmill, thus perpetuating the reality of being separate. In fact, that's how the 'operating system' of the reality of separation is perpetuated—by the belief systems that hold it in place.

None of this was ever your fault.

2

The Language of Creation

Discovering the Language of Creation

In my own search to escape suffering, I discovered that the more I became aware of how I operated, how I was designed, and how I connected with life, the more alive, inspirited, I became.

Reminding myself that the very fact that I did consults for people gave me the air that I knew, they didn't, encouraged me to develop a skill set that awakened in people their own listening. I learned how to deflect the tendency toward listening to me and learned how to support people in awakening more and more to the magic of their own listening.

As the mystical nature of me matured and I saw the impact on people's lives through the work I did, I gained strength in my own listening to what was needed in a consult. I became adept at moving into the cellular resonance of *them* speaking to *themselves* through my voice. Feeling the cellular quickening of the resonance of their core design, not my interpretation of their design, I recognized the magic of awakening inherent in each person. I sometimes flooded with the alchemy of life as their Original Design activated and I knew what had separated them from themselves, would separate them no more and they were being freed to discover themselves as whole.

I dug in. One of the most important aspects of our existence is to get savvy about the extent of the problem that is before us. Everywhere I looked, I saw how we had been entrained since birth and quite possibly before, to not look within ourselves for ourselves. We looked in books, in religion, and in education. We looked anywhere, everywhere, and to everyone for what we were designed to be, but not inside ourselves.

To add insult to injury, underneath this despicable misperception of where our truth existed, was an actual cellular, leathery lethargy that did not let in the light, energy, accurate information, or any form of self-awareness. It was as if we have been literally cut off from the life giving force that had created us.

Over the years of quickening the design of the people I worked with, I began to awaken into how to transfer to them the life giving force that I had bonded with in my own journey to survive mentally, emotionally, and physically. I concentrated on how to transfer that to others and I awoke into an amazing discovery.

Behind our words and our actions was a force that we as living beings shared. Some people called it the void, the emptiness, the nothingness. I recognized that it was this that I was referring to in my humorous quip, when people asked me what I channeled, "I channel you. I listen to the nothing and in the nothing the language of you rises." All of existence carries a wordless language of connection and everything is created to exist in harmony, grace, and the power of manifestation in incomprehensible complex matrices of connection. We weren't designed to manifest just 'any ole thing'. We were designed to manifest the magnificent beingness of our own part of the great living all-ness of where everything came from. And that in that beingness, we lived as what was ours to be, ours to do, ours to have.

Knowing, as we crossed into the year 2000, that over the next decade, enough people had to cross the bridge into their own knowing for the species to survive, I needed to make sure that happened. The ability to think with our own mind was essential. Yet the opportunity for human beings being conscious of their part in the shift of what was happening was now the emerging gift of our human birthright. Knowing that, I knew my job was part of a fantastic opening that had been forecast since ancient times, I knew I needed to organize everything I was doing so people could be supported in becoming rapidly 'self' aware. In the awareness of the design of their being, their selfhood could rise. Connected with their life force energy and living intelligence of Creation, the new realities they came here to create would be born.

> People needed to become their own Original Design. They
> were needed for the future calling.

The clarity and urgency of my knowing paid off. I live a life of manifestation that does not happen within the rational mind, only within the mind of Creation. But the opening of the doorway into what would become a vital part of what shifted people into their own awakening, blew my mind. Creation delivered.

A client called me and asked me to meet with him. Having done consults with me, he also had investigated what was it that had the consults be so impactful? Who would have thought?! He talked to me about quantum physics, resonance, the Golden Spiral, the Fibonacci Sequencing. He had created what he could figure out about how to create a language that manifested the quantum mind. I felt like we were scientists convening on the verge of a huge breakthrough. He had done his research. While the syntax of the quantum language did not provide the awakening of the being of the human being, it did let you peer into the quantum mind. Figuring out the flaws, having enough information now to see how to construct direct access to one's being through language, I began.

I knew that I had discovered a Language of Connection. I had a way to have people begin to connect to the unique and essential aspect of Creation they were. I knew I could exercise their mind and restore their neural synapses. It was a formula for becoming self-aware and finally embodying what they were truly designed to be.

Like an engine hose disconnected from the oil, the car cannot get what it needs to run. We, with our neural networks disconnected from Creation, cannot operate as ourselves. We become prey to others' beliefs and understandings.

What is it to think, not just have thought? A generator of thought, not just a receiver?

What is it to think within the mind of Creation? To think with the mind that created us? To think with Creation?

I knew thinking as part of a quantum field activated manifestation that corresponded to what each person came to fulfill as a living being.

I am not speaking of fulfilling suffering. I am talking about fulfilling what Creation created us to be, to do, and to have. That is the essence of fulfillment.

> What I read in a person is the Template that each person
> came to be, the true potentiality of a Human Being, their
> Original Design.

Those DNA Templates are as juicy and lively as the feisty squirrel and regal buck and as multi-hued and dynamically colorful as the land, the skies, and the seas.

I knew that I had the key to giving people a way to reconnect to the mind of their design that is never separated from Creation.

I created language Templates that would restore the matrix of each person's direct connection to the greater matrix of creation. The exercises created from these Templates would reveal to each human being what was unique and essential about them. Then I test ran it for two years.

The results were astounding. The test group began to discern two mindscapes: One mindscape that looped and looped, not able to resolve any issue effectively and another mindscape that could see the landscape of everything occurring . . . 'everything made sense'. The Creation Exercises were born. Each person discovered what to be, do, and have as well as finding themselves naturally doing what there was to do, being what there was to be and having what there was to have. Reality began to mirror what internally people had felt they truly were and what they truly felt was real. Soon the discomfort of the mind that took them down the tube of confusion and suffering was so revolting that people lived to do the exercises.

Over time as people's lives re-oriented through what they wrote, they would say, "This is the life I was meant to have." Things lined up. Connections came out of the blue that had had no hope of happening before. Results started to occur in ways that could not be explained. Life just started responding. People found they were moving with life and life was moving with them . . . no longer separated from what they were always designed to be. They became their own version of extraordinary.

For many years, I wrote the language exercises on my health. Now, while many years may seem like a long melee, it wasn't. While awareness is balm to the soul, clarity is also required for life to manifest what is actually needed. That clarity sometimes takes time. However the movement from dysfunction to function, from illness to health, from life not working to life working[4] was powerful and life altering as I peeled away the layers between what I wasn't and what I was. What I was after was what had my body stay heavy, what was the source of the confusing energetic states that I went through sometimes leaving me 'mostly dead', and what was the extraordinary awareness that birthed in me after going through these collapses.

Before beginning the Creation Exercises, practitioners, physicians and trainings had helped me cope with my body for many years with no visible success. After I began the exercises, my mind opened up beyond what was considered possible into a 'meta[5]-reality' where the impossible and improbable found root and things began to come together . . . fast. The exercises activated the broader mindscape of what was going on. The clarity of what my true design as a body became 'self-evident'. I became self-aware. I stopped trying to just get better. I knew what needed to happen. I knew what for me was real, where my problems were sourced from, and the true nature of what my body was for me.

I remembered in a way that could not be denied.

I knew I needed to discover what had my body and my soul, my flesh and my spirit, embody as one.

_____

[4]   The phrase 'life working' is distinct in the meta-language that Tantra created. 'Life working' is where things come together the way you always knew they could.

[5]   Meta means to include and go beyond.

This book is designed to give you a passageway back into
a language that holds the magnificence of your Original
Design: The Language of Creation itself.

Language is a template of expression within which reality occurs. We
see, sense, think, feel, hear, and are well or not well, according to how
language organizes our reality. In modern times, language is limited to
the spoken and written word, but language existed long before speaking
and writing began. Language did not just generate from the need to
connect with fellow humans. Language once generated from the desire
to connect with the greater reality ancient humans knew they were a
part of. These humans knew themselves as part of the creative process
of Creation. Ancient language, whether verbal or artful, connected
human beings with Creation. Before humanity began to form thought
into belief, language let Creation move through the human experience
and human beings expressed their lives in connection with Creation. We
see this in Sanskrit. It is a language that is not based on explanation or
understanding but on resonance.

Within us lies a Language of Creation that exists both internally
and externally in our attempt to be connected to the Universe, to
ourselves, and to each other. Whether we express ourselves skillfully or
clumsily, an ancient language seeks to rise within us where we experience
ourselves as part of Creation in thought, word, and deed. Realities are
created by the Language of Creation. What is present in the language
of one reality is not present in the language of another. We see this
in multiple personalities. One personality can have a deadly allergy.
Another personality will not. Our internal language shapes our thoughts.
Thoughts shape our reality. We see this in what some people hold to be
fantasy and others hold to be real.

What if we could return to the Language of Creation where our
direct connection to Creation gave us access to what was ours to create
and we could become creators of realities that have only until now, lived
in our dreams?

Before teaching you the actual Creation Exercises, let's first look at how the Creation Exercises generate thought that gives you access to the thought process of Creation.

The Language of Creation is connection-oriented and gives us direct access to our experience, creating a connection where we can include more and more, increasing our connection to ourselves, the world, Creation, and each other.

When you think in the Language of Creation:

1. You can think with the creative power of what you were thinking.
2. You find yourself present to what you are thinking, like being on a mindscape where life is visible within the clarity of your thoughts.
3. You no longer think for or against. You think with.
4. You no longer think either/or, you think both/and.
5. You no longer think good or bad, right or wrong. You think, as Rumi says, "In the playing field beyond all right or wrong doing."
6. You find you can include everything, nothing excluded, synthesizing your thoughts into whole system thinking[6] naturally.
7. You no longer have to explain or understand what you think. What you are thinking is so part of you and is so present for you, you transmit to others what you are present to from your connection to it.

Instead of parroting knowledge, you are aware of your direct connection to life and speak from that connection. Your thoughts become life generating and life enhancing. You become self-aware.

---

[6]   Whole-systems thinking synthesizes the interrelationships of what you are aware of so you arrive at conclusions and solutions different from those constructed from a conditioned range of focus. Considering the constituting parts of a system rather than narrowly focusing on the parts themselves.

The Language of Creation moves with Creation in your thoughts, aligning you thought by thought with what is yours to do, be, and have. You no longer have to prove yourself to know you are of value.

As the world is changing, you need direct access to what is unfolding that you have no past experience of. The Language of Creation is a metalanguage—a language that includes what you are now and goes beyond into what you are becoming. In a metalanguage, what you say transmits your awareness without the need to explain. Why? Because when the experience is present for you when you communicate, the resonance of that experience supersedes the words.

The Language of Creation is a resonant field connected to your reality. Your words carry connection not disconnection. Your thinking makes you part of your reality instead of separating you from it. Your reality carries language.

Your reality that you access through this Language of Creation is:

1. The reality that connects you to the essence of what it is for you to be alive and exist as whole.
2. The reality that manifests the fulfillment of what you are actually designed to be.
3. The reality that awakens you into your unique and essential connection to all of life.

3

The Creation Exercises

The Creation Exercises are named such because doing
these exercises restores your connection to Creation.
Without that connection, you can never know your
Original Design.

The Framework of the Creation Exercises

The framework of the Creation Exercises is based on an ancient formula
of Creation. Our ancient ancestors created formulas based on the design
of Creation so that their physical manifestations carried the life force
energy that created the universe.

What is Creation?

For me, since I was very, very young, I have been in the experience
of what I would call the greater intelligence of our existence. Mostly,
when we use the word *intelligence* we think of the word *intellect*. I don't
mean intellect. I mean a living, breathing, vibrating resonant universal
consciousness that is active. That active universal consciousness that
makes up our existence I call Creation. Creation is made up of a myriad
of realities born of the creative process. Everything created is a reflection
of Creation. Creation is an active intelligence wherein creation occurs.
We are a product of Creation. Therefore we have the same intelligence as
Creation, each in our unique and individuated design.

This is what we are. We are part of a great living intelligence. We
are part of this great living energy of life. We are designed to reflect
on ourselves and gain recognition of ourselves through experience.
When we restore this intelligence in us and discover that our design is
as a unique and essential aspect of this intelligence of Creation, we are
present to a fuller spectrum of ourselves and our experience. We begin to

know that every moment of our life, every day of our life is a reflection of Creation. We reflect upon our days as part of the intelligence of Creation. We are present to our lives as part of the activity of Creation. We recognize and become awake to the multi-faceted dynamic design of what we truly are.

The ancients comprehended this principle of Creation and their languages, their sciences, their engineering, their religions, etc., reflected this. A fundamental structure of Creation that has been remembered through time is the principle of the Golden Spiral, in modern times resurrected as the Fibonacci Sequence[7].

The Fibonacci Sequence

When you write the Creation Exercises, you are writing three sentences four times. The wording overlaps. This overlap creates the sequencing found in the Fibonacci Sequence . . . a math of connection.

0, 1, 1, 2, 3, 5, 8, 13, 21, 34, 55, 89, 144 . . . .

A mathematician, Fibonacci, discovered this mathematical sequence in the western world, but it appeared long before Fibonacci in Eastern Indian mathematics. Indian mathematics were based on the formula of Creation long before English and Western languages were formed.

In our western world, the sequencing shows up in the 400 BCs as the Golden Ratio, the Golden Mean, and the Golden Spiral. The Greeks brought the Golden Ratio into their science, their architecture, and their art. The Greeks based their quality of life on the principle that life is designed to be beautiful, aesthetically pleasing, and the reflection of the human soul born of Creation.

The alchemy of energy and spirit were sciences deeply studied and applied by advanced civilizations: the Mayans, the Egyptians,

---

[7]   By definition, the first two numbers in the Fibonacci sequence are 0 and 1, and each subsequent number is the sum of the previous two.

the Orientals, the Eastern traditions and the Greeks. Our modern civilizations lost touch with these ancient alchemies, yet without our realizing it we find the Golden Spiral everywhere from a sunflower to a conch shell, from the small bone in our ear to our DNA. What is amazing is every human being's DNA is shaped by this sequencing.

We are composed of and by the Golden Spiral. Our very physical being and nature reflect the living sequencing of manifestation found in Creation.

The Wording of the Creation Exercises

The words used in the Creation Exercises were formed from a framework of language that, through two distinctly designed Templates, reconnects the spirit and flesh and brain and mind of a human being. One Template design organizes your thoughts consistent with how the physical plane works. The other Template organizes your thoughts consistent with how the non-physical plane works. A human being is an operating system that is heaven and earth, form and formless, matter and energy as well as brain and mind, spirit and flesh, biochemical and alchemical. We are both. We were not designed to ignore the flesh and seek the spirit. Our spirit and flesh are the composite of embodiment that we are . . . both majestic and brilliant in their design. Our thoughts are not designed to just spit out random thought dictated by our life experience. Our thoughts are also stimulated from the mind of Creation. That is why mystics like me hear God, a vibration of consciousness that goes beyond the reality we were born into.

When our thoughts are too lofty and existential, we actually have trouble with activity of everyday life. When our body is only running on adrenaline, we wear out. The brain and the mind are designed to function in an accordion of capability from being diffused and one with all life to being able to focus on details and solve complex problems. The Creation Exercises restore this accordion capability. For me, I was too diffused always hanging out in the mind of God. When I began the exercises, almost all of a sudden I could read directions for my computer, think about what I needed to buy for groceries. Other people, so literal and fixed in the everyday, begin to experience a broader spectrum of experience.

The Creation Exercises are a modern form of an ancient syntax of Creation that connect the form and the formless, brain and the mind, energy and the matter, flesh and spirit—the full form of what a human being is designed to be.

We were created as a meta-structure of brain/mind and flesh/spirit. Our energy/matter being is designed to operate as one . . . in oneness. Together as a whole system, the unity point, the metapoint of brain/ mind and flesh/spirit synthesizes information within which reality is created. Without our energy/matter being, operating as a whole system, the information cannot synthesize and move in a sequencing progression from awareness to manifestation. When the physical and non-physical information cannot synthesize, the mind and body stop functioning properly and the human being is unable to fulfill on the input from Creation.

The Language of Creation is both physical and non-physical. Imagine what it would be like to think with both your mind and your spirit . . . to be one with the Universe one minute and run the business of life the next.

The Vibration of the Creation Exercises

Language, based on the mathematical structure of the Golden Spiral such as Sanskrit, began as an oral tradition that through its language structure kept its people in unity with Creation. Used in the Vedas and in the Eastern tradition of Hinduism and Buddhism, this oral mathematical language chanted the sounds of God or the Divine so that the vibration of Creation was the source of what created their lives.

The backbone of Eastern belief is that we were formed out of the formless through sound into form . . . the alchemy of energy and spirit. Language began as sound . . . resonance. When you are doing the exercises, you are listening for the sound of Creation. Through using this resonant language you restore your ability to exist in the sound and vibration that created our Universe, our Earth, and us. Your Original Design only operates in resonance with Creation. As your capacity for resonance increases, you begin to experience being part of everything that exists, in resonance with Creation. Restoring your Original Design through the languaging of the exercises, you move in resonance with what is yours to do, yours to be, and yours to have.

> The restoration of your Original Design, your ability to
> move in resonance with Creation and naturally move with
> what is yours to do, be, and have is the phenomenon that
> happens when you do the Creation Exercises.

While you will experience a state shift in reality by simply reading and absorbing the information in this book, learning the Creation Exercises is essential to shift you from one state of reality to another.

The Templates

The Creation Exercises have two Templates each:

1. A Craving Template.
2. An Observing Template.

You will be learning two Creation Exercises in this book:

1. The *Craving* Creation Exercise.
2. The *Craving Being* Creation Exercise.

In this book, the Creation Exercises use four basic Templates designed to restore your own unique connection to Creation. Using these Templates, your brain can 'reconnect the dots' so your thoughts no longer spin out into nothingness or loop incessantly. Your thoughts begin to shape the reality that exists when you are connected to Creation . . . your natural reality.

The Templates are structured to actualize the restoration of your full intelligence, which is your mind when it is reconnected to the greater intelligence from which everything comes into existence. Using these Templates in the Creation Exercises, you shift from a reality of separation into a reality of unity.

Your brainwaves oscillate at different vibrational rates, inducing thoughts and experiences that affect your daily survival, stimulate your dreamtime, lift you into transcendent states of knowing, give you the ability to enter into meditation, and can even bring you into oneness with what created you. The four Templates stimulate the oscillating rates of the brain opening up portals to higher vibration brain states. Then in adding your words to words of the Templates in the Creation Exercises, you find you can think in higher vibrational states, you can see what you couldn't see, know what you couldn't know, and solve what you couldn't solve.

> "We can't solve problems by using the same kind of
> thinking we used when we created them."
>
> Albert Einstein

These Templates used in the Creation Exercises are designed to keep you in a co-creative process with Creation.

The Results of doing the Creation Exercises

Ongoing, as you do the exercises, more and more fear, anxiety, and panic subside. You move more gracefully with transition. Circumstances begin to align with your inner vision. You sustain and maintain the broader view of your higher mind. What was once hoped for begins to manifest and the reality you feel part of, begins to become a stable and normal part of your existence, and much, much more.

When you reactivate the two aspects of the Language of Creation, a metapoint occurs. A metapoint is a point of unity. It is often referred to as zero point or still point. The metapoint is where the physical/non-physical, matter/energy, flesh/spirit come together as a whole system and you get access to Creation where all possibility and an inconceivable source of energy exist.

As you do the Creation Exercises, your journey on Earth becomes a metapoint, a unifying point where you can, in the miracle of your design, go past the physical into the non-physical in varying degrees of unity. Doing the Creation Exercises you anchor your basic connection to Creation where fundamental needs can be met. Continuing to do them, you embody varying degrees of unity between your spirit and flesh gaining more and more capacity for higher mind and more transcendent states of being. Using the Craving Templates in conjunction with the Observing Templates you evolve into your complete form, your embodiment—the metapoint of spirit and flesh, human and being.

The Language of the Physical/ Non-Physical, Matter/ Energy, Flesh/Spirit

The first part of the Language of Creation we are going to explore is the language of matter, of flesh, of form, the physical, etc. We will explore craving. Then we will learn the language of energy, spirit, being, the formless, the non-physical, etc. We will explore observing. Used together, they activate our innate wholeness where self-awareness and self-actualization are systemically restored to a seamless ease and grace of living.

Exercising the Language of Creation in this book unifies your system of energy with your system of matter. The energetic alignment in this metalanguage powerfully affects the unifying points, the metapoints, of three areas of your energy/matter embodiment: the nervous system and the quantum field of Creation, the solar plexus and the solar chakra, the brain and the third eye.

BREATHE

Meditation

Begin with this short meditative breathing so you can take in the information with greater ease:

[Breathe in]
I am the embodiment of the non-physical and the physical,
[Breathe out]

[Breathe in]
I am spirit and flesh, matter and energy.
[Breathe out]

[Breathe in]
I am both a Human
[Breathe out]

[Breathe in]
And a Being,
[Breathe out]

[Breathe in]
Both Cosmic and Earthly,
[Breathe out]

[Breathe in]
Both infinite and finite,
[Breathe out]

[Breathe in]
Both immortal and mortal,
[Breathe out]

[Breathe in]
Both eternal and temporal.
[Breathe out]

You as the Craver

The Miracle of Your Physical Form

The Creation Exercises you will be learning are designed to activate very specific areas of your physical body and your energy being. The nervous system and the solar system are interacted with because these areas elicit reaction instead of response. We are so dulled down that as we begin to awaken and our nervous system and our solar plexus are stimulated, we fear and shut down our own awakening. While we do not have the experience of our brain reacting, the neural-pathways of our brain have been compromised—we cannot hear the unity of our spirit/flesh, brain/mind system. We cannot process and integrate the complete information that gives us access to the awareness, the fullness—the complete spectrum of our lives.

The Nervous System

The nervous system is the physical receiver of energy whether it is adrenalin or the energy from the Universe. Our nervous systems are critical at this time of our awakening. The vibration of the Earth is rising. The blockages of trauma that kept our vibration low and kept our spirit and our flesh unable to communicate are dissolving. Our nervous systems, as essential receptors of the energy of Creation, are coming back online. We are now at the effect of powerful amounts of energy moving through us. Our physical bodies have been dormant, lethargic, leaving our nervous systems weak, unable to process successfully the energy moving through it. With our nervous systems unable to handle the power of the Universe that we are part of, our bodies collapse or are strung out. It is as simple as that. When there is no place for the energy to go, the energy becomes disruptive.

The cellular trauma, passed down from generation to generation, froze our nerves in place so our overtaxed emotions tsunami through our unstable nerve system. Yet the more energy of Creation our nervous systems can take in, the more stamina we have to embody our unique connection to Creation.

The Solar Plexus

The solar plexus is sometimes called the abdominal brain. The solar plexus is a mass of nerves composed of the same gray and white nervous substance or brain matter similar to that found in the brain. When the solar plexus is injured, our entire physical system is seriously affected. After a severe, shocking injury, death can often ensue.

The word solar comes from its central position in the body, as well as the fact that the filaments of the solar plexus reach in all directions like the rays of the sun. These filaments stretch toward the important abdominal organs and also into the filaments of the aorta.

Just as the sun is the great powerhouse and reservoir of energy for our solar system, the solar plexus is the great reservoir for our physical life force.

Our solar plexus governs the sympathetic nervous system which regulates and energizes respiration, circulation, and digestive functions upon which your physical life depends.

This abdominal brain is found fully formed and perfect, and even performs some important functions when the human embryo is at an early stage while the brain in our skull is a mere pulpy mass, incapable of performing any function whatsoever.

Oriental physicians who lived centuries ago recognized the solar plexus as the seat of a human being's emotional nature. While our culture has held the heart to be the center of our emotional nature, in reality it is the solar plexus that is the great center of the sympathetic nervous system.

There is an important relationship between our emotional states and our solar plexus. It is hard to feel confident or loving when fear, dread, and suspense carry a sinking or sick feeling in your gut. You find it difficult to be at ease when you have butterflies in the pit of your stomach.

Our emotions are far more primitive and fundamental to our nature than ideas and were central to our evolution long before we developed our 'thinking brain'.

The solar plexus is where all our strong and elemental feelings rise. They flow from the solar plexus influencing our heart's ability to express love. Gut feelings of doubt, unworthiness, fear of future all rise from the solar plexus. We have trouble trusting what our heart is showing us . . . the love we came here to receive and express. Without the solar plexus being calm and receiving the information from Creation that that person, that job, that direction is ours to have, to be, to do, we cannot express our heart. We react instead of respond shutting the door on the deep experiences we came here to have.

The pervasive disturbance of these times is the activity of our flesh/spirit, matter/energy systems restoring. Awakening the fundamental intelligence of the solar plexus is essential to this restoration! Through awakening this fundamental intelligence, our emotional nature moves with our connection to Creation, not in reaction to it.

The Brain

The brain is the central operating system of the physical body and is close to the sensory systems of vision, hearing, balance, taste, and smell. The brain is complex. The cerebral cortex contains about 15-33 billion neurons. Each neuron is connected by synapses to several thousand other neurons. This is what is referred to as the neural-synapses of the brain. Physiologically, the brain controls the other organs of the body through generating muscle activity and hormones. Centralized control in the brain allows us to move rapidly with coordination when any changes in our environment occur. A human being has sophisticated, purposeful control because of the information-integrating capabilities of a centralized brain.

In philosophy, the brain has been designated as where the mind lives in the physical plane and yet even in modern neuroscience, thought and consciousness coming from brain activity is difficult to comprehend.

As we begin to realize that we are the metapoint of the physical and non-physical plane, we will realize that the pulpy mass in our skull is matter and energy, brain and mind.

The brain and the mind exemplify the unity of the spirit and the flesh, the matter and energy system that we are. As our matter/energy, spirit/flesh, physical/non-physical metapoints are restored, we have the full function of actualization, manifestation, and fulfillment.

One of the discoveries that has dashed any thought that we are limited by our matter is the discovery of the neuroplasticity of the brain. The one thing I don't want you to miss here is that the spirit is not governed by the flesh. We were all energy before matter. The physical laws are fixed to keep everything operating properly in the physical plane. The non-physical laws are pure potential governed by Creation itself and our part of it. That means our mind is energy and that energy can create an influence on the physical plane.

Neuroplasticity speaks to this.

The belief, until recently, that the brain is hardwired and that the neurons in your brain die, has been proven false. This belief came from the old science that looked at the Universe and a human being as a machine. Now we know that when one part of the brain isn't working, another part of the brain can take it over. This is part of what happened to me when I was a teenager. From an early age, I experienced reality very differently than the people around me. I saw things, I felt things and I experienced things that others didn't. At sixteen, I began to experience myself in two places at the same time. This was the first time that was going to be one of many, when the reality I thought was real, was not the only reality going on. I made the mistake of sharing it with my mother and was rushed off to the psychiatric department of our small Tennessee hospital. My Episcopal minister, Papa Kent, who had been my spiritual friend from the age of five, stopped my mother from giving me shock treatment. He also found an amazing psychiatrist, Dr. White, who refused to medicate me and, instead, taught me how to move through my brain and interact with it. I needed to rewire some of the gaps I had between the reality I lived in, with my parents, and the reality I lived in where my parents and most other people, did not. Dr. White and Papa Kent birthed a mystic . . . me.

Years later, I was asked to come to Scotland to work with a young girl between eight and ten who was having visions, some of which gave her terrible nightmares. Her mother had taken her to a neurologist and he recommended giving her a drug to deaden part of her brain. She had agreed. The result was the visions did not stop and the child began to have deadly seizures.

Having had deep personal interactions with my brain for such a long time, when the mother asked me if I would speak with her daughter and try to help her, I said yes. This was long before the thinking that we could rewire our brain was even available. The seizures were happening about every three hours. In Scotland sitting by this precious emaciated young child, I waited until a seizure was over and asked her to talk to me about what was happening in her brain. She responded immediately. She had abilities like mine to be in touch with the deeper nature of things. I could see she was a budding talent. We walked and talked about what she had been experiencing. I shared with her what it was like for me when I was her age, especially about what I called the outside nightmares and what she called her painful visions. I told her that when young, the psychic mind develops seeing things both outside and inside. I told her my worst one was a shark that swam toward me about the level of my pillow when I woke in the morning. We laughed.

Back in her room with her mother, I stayed with her as the next few seizures came on. Before each seizure, we worked together until she could track what she was experiencing in the neural-synapses of her brain. Then in the three hour interval after the next seizure, we tracked how she felt before she blacked out. In her amazing perceptive way, she became aware of where the seizures were triggering in her brain.

Over the next few days she found where she could reroute the energy moving toward the destroyed part of her brain, where they had damaged her brain tissue. The seizures decreased in danger and were less frequent. About twenty years later, I got a postcard in the mail from her: "My brain is all the way back. I am working with children now who have intuitive talent. I love helping them with the learning curves and growing pains that come with their talent. I love you."

Norman Doidge, in his book *The Brain That Changes Itself* [8], brilliantly describes the new scoop on the brain. The brain can reorganize and restructure itself. New brain cells are created unceasingly. Your brain is designed to take over functions that are needed when part of the body is compromised, for instance your knee circuitry can expand to take over the arm functions. How amazing is that?

Much of the cellular complexes operate as a hologram, as in everything is connected to everything else. A cellular biologist, Bruce Lipton, in his book *The Biology of Belief* [9], provides evidence that through thinking and other brain activities we can actualize reality through the DNA encoding in our bodies. We can literally share our brain's anatomy to shift our behavior; even grow a new version of ourselves!

In the introduction to *The Brain That Changes Itself*, Doidge writes, "In my travels, I met a scientist who enabled people who had been blind since birth to see, another who enabled the deaf to hear. I met people whose learning disorders were cured and whose IQs were raised. I saw evidence that it is possible for eighty year olds to sharpen their memories to function the way they did when they were fifty-five. I saw people rewire their brains with their thoughts, to cure previously incurable obsessions and traumas."

Mostly, up until now, not knowing we are part of an intricate and highly developed system of Creation, we have been adrift on an insufficient informational sea. What if we had a way to apply what the Norman Doidges and Bruce Liptons of the world told us?

---

[8]   Doidge, N., & MD. (2007). *The Brain That Changes Itself.* New York: Penguin Group.

[9]   Lipton, B. H. (2005). *The Biology of Belief: Unleashing The Power of Consciousness, Matter and Miracles.* Santa Rosa, CA: Mountain of Love/ Elite Books.

This is just a taste of what is occurring. We do not know what life will be like for us as our systems come back online. What we do know is our physical form is part of what is happening and needs not only a tune-up but a reboot to get going.

The Design of the Craving Template

There is a basic principle that causes all matter to come
into existence. That basic principle of the physical is
Craving.

This is the source of all physical intelligence. A human being is a metapoint, a connecting point of the Cosmos and the Earth, the spirit and the flesh, matter and energy, form and formless. The Earth and our flesh both crave physical existence. Physical matter is formed by this craving. This craving is what causes everything on Earth to be brought into form.

The seed pushes through the ground. What causes that push is the seed's innate need for the sun. That innate need awakens a powerful craving within the physical intelligence of the seed. The seed's craving of the sun, its need to live and stay alive forces the plant into physical form.

The physical intelligence of our matter causes the sperm to crave the egg. Our conception is our physiological craving to come into physical existence.

The Craving Template is designed by the physical
intelligence that creates physical manifestation on Earth.

Craving creates: Craving is the urge that brings life into form on this planet. We feel the power of craving in our gut, our solar plexus. Our biological cravings come from being part of the Great Living Intelligence of Creation. Our nervous system quivers alive with our anticipation. We get our messages from the Cosmos through what we crave. Our cravings are part of a universal communication system within which every human being receives the stimulus of their unique and essential design.

Creating sustains and maintains: Whatever is created from the initial craving stimulus must be able to sustain and maintain its physical form to stay in existence. A craving, sustained and maintained, becomes a manifestation of our Physical Creation.

Sustaining and maintaining embodies: At some point when something can sustain and maintain long enough, it embodies. The Earth becomes a planet. The seed becomes a flower, a tree, a plant. The embryo becomes a baby. What you seek to manifest not only comes into reality, but comes into reality in a way that keeps it in existence. Humanity can, to some level, bring things into existence . . . a child, a job, a marriage but these acts of manifestation do not stay true to what we envisioned them to be. When you are manifesting from your direct connection to Creation, what you envisioned stays in existence.

To embody: Here on Earth, when multiple systems become able to function, automatically organic matter becomes embodied as a whole system response. The Earth is an embodied being. The Earth has ecosystems that automatically sustain and maintain themselves. The Earth doesn't have to start all over again every morning.

Your body has biological systems that automatically sustain and maintain themselves. You are an embodied being, a whole system response. You don't have to wake up in the morning and say, "Heart beat! Lungs breathe!" This is the great mystery of life—we are self-sustaining and self-maintaining systems that do not go out of existence until our ability to self-sustain and self-maintain breaks down. We are matter embodied on the physical plane that inherently, if fed, sheltered, and watered, sustain and maintain our ability to live here.

We are in a period of human history where the trauma that keeps us in reaction and on high alert is breaking down the automatic systems within us that keep our physical matter vital and in existence. The solar plexus, when functioning properly, keeps our fundamental survival systems going. We must have it stay calm and only react when we are in real danger, not the constant imagined danger we have become encultured into. Presently we are trapped in the reaction of our solar plexus. This is a disconnection between our spirit and our flesh. We are trapped in reaction, fight or flight, screw it or kill it, the biochemical response to fear. We are stuck in protect or defend. This is what we are left with when our flesh is not responsive to the intelligence of our spirit.

The Craving part of the Creation Exercise is designed to calm the solar plexus by you directing the energy of fear, anxiety, and reaction into what you want to use that energy to create.

Reaction gives way to response. You begin to be able to direct the released energy toward the manifestation you crave whether it is love, well-being, success, or being one with the Divine.

The Craving part of the Creation Exercise guides your
cravings toward a desired manifestation.

Let's begin.

This first level of the Creation Exercises restores your direct connection with Creation, where you begin to experience Creation responding to and beginning to manifest what you crave. Each Exercise increases the intelligence of craving and how craving brings what you crave into existence. Craving is only half of what you are. Remember, you are the metapoint of physical and non-physical existence. Let's begin discovering who you are as a craver.

You were born to crave! Everything physical is designed to crave. Your ability to create is directly related to how powerfully you can crave and not suffer from your craving. The Craving Templates are designed to have your solar plexus stop reacting and your nervous system stay calm as the power of craving moves through you. When your solar plexus stops reacting, your nervous system is free to respond and the neural-synapses of your brain begin processing the thought manifestation of Creation. As you begin to do the Craving aspect of the exercise, you discover that when you crave powerfully an amazing phenomenon occurs. Manifestation rises to meet you in ways you could never have imagined.

YOUR MATTER MATTERS!

TEMPLATE 1 CRAVING

Before beginning to read the guidelines on the next page, please write out the Template below on lined paper. (You can also download the Templates from iuwcinstitute.com/tmps in a print-friendly format.) Use this to guide you in doing the Craving Creation Exercise.

DO NOT WRITE ON THIS TEMPLATE. When doing the Templates you must write out each word on a separate piece of paper.

It is best to practice these Templates writing long hand, but if you find writing tedious, using a computer is satisfactory.

This CRAVING Template focuses on what you truly crave. Cravings A1, A2, A3 can be all the same or after a month you may put something different as A1, A2, A3 after each *Craving*.

CI:
Craving $A1$ creates $B1$.
Creating $B1$ sustains and maintains $C1$.
Sustaining and maintaining $C1$ embodies $X1$.

CII:
Craving $A1$ or $A2$ creates $B2$.
Creating $B2$ sustains and maintains $C2$.
Sustaining and maintaining $C2$ embodies $X2$.

CIII:
Craving $A1$ or $A3$ creates $B3$.
Creating $B3$ sustains and maintains $C3$.
Sustaining and maintaining $C3$ embodies $X3$.

CC:*
Craving $X1$ creates $X2$.
Creating $X2$ sustains and maintains $X3$.
Sustaining and maintaining $X3$ embodies XX.

TEMPLATE 1 CRAVING GUIDELINES

Now let's begin the first part of your Craving Creation Exercise.

Remember the Craving is only one half of the Creation Exercises so keep the Craving[s] you write so you can finish them after you learn how to do the Observing part of the exercise. Remember the Craving and Observing Templates are both needed for you to have completed your Creation Exercise.

Craving <u>A</u> (CRAVE SOMETHING YOU TRULY CRAVE)

Almost all of humanity has forgotten the power of craving. Often, in the misunderstanding of spiritual disciplines, we think that craving is greedy, a sin, or a lie.

This is not so. You are organic. You are designed to crave like the seed craves the sun and the sperm craves the egg.

Example: Craving <u>love</u> [<u>A1</u>]

Craving <u>A1</u> creates <u>B1</u>.

What do you want (what you crave) to create? Really think. Thinking of what you *crave creating* in a pleasant, harmonic, and life-enhancing way resets your life and your experience of living.

Everything must be what you want, not what *might* be your present experience, i.e., Craving <u>love</u> creates <u>pain</u>. Ask yourself: Do I really want love to create pain? What *do* I want love to create?

WHAT YOU CRAVE TO CREATE MUST BE PLEASANT, RESONANT, AND SOMETHING YOU TRULY WANT TO CREATE.

To be resonant is to have something be pleasant, life-enhancing, and harmonic.

Example: Craving <u>love</u> [A1] creates <u>joy</u>. [B1]

What you write doesn't have to be logical or even make sense. You only need to write what is pleasant, harmonic, life-enhancing, and resonates—something you want. Creation does the rest!

Breathe.

Do not think too much. Take the first word or phrase that comes to mind that is pleasant.

Do not worry if you can't think what to write. Your brain is locked in a grid of traumatized neurons.

Keep reading the statements: What do I crave? What do I want that I crave to create? Your neurons will start *firing* on behalf of what aligns you with Creation. Your mind will burst open. Sometimes when this happens, you may get emotional . . . cry or feel elated. Sometimes you may even feel a little frightened or nervous. This is your solar plexus coming back online in alignment with Creation. Perhaps this is the first time you've ever considered what you crave can create, move with it gently, like you would if doing a physical exercise for the first time.

Creating <u>B1</u> sustains and maintains <u>C1</u>. REPEAT THE PATTERN
EXACTLY.

B1 must be written exactly as it was written at the end of the *Craving* sentence, and at the beginning of the *Creating* sentence.

Examples:

> Craving <u>love</u> [A1] creates <u>joy</u> [B1].
> Creating <u>joy</u> [B1] sustains and maintains <u>authentic companionship</u> [C1].

YOU MUST **NOT** USE THE SAME EXACT WORD OR PHRASE MORE THAN ONCE. You are, however, welcome to embellish.

2 Examples:

Craving <u>a new job</u> creates <u>excitement</u>.
Creating <u>excitement</u> sustains and maintains <u>a world of excitement</u>
<u>I have never known.</u>
Craving <u>health</u> creates <u>vitality</u>.
Creating <u>vitality</u> sustains and maintains <u>new openings for vitality</u>.

Remember, in Creation, much can be craved and much can be created without lasting very long. The Creation Exercises are designed not only for you to create but also for what you have created to be sustainable: to be sustained and maintained.

Sustaining and maintaining <u>C1</u> embodies <u>X1</u>.

Example:

Craving <u>love</u> [A1] creates <u>joy</u> [B1].
Creating <u>joy</u> [B1] sustains and maintains <u>authentic companionship.</u>
[C1]
Sustaining and maintaining <u>authentic companionship</u> [C1] embodies
<u>heaven</u> [X1].

The ultimate goal in life is to create something that can sustain and maintain itself long enough to embody.

Human beings were designed to self-sustain and self-maintain. That means that self-sustaining and self-maintaining is part of your design. You are designed, as the Irish say, for "The road to rise up to meet you." This means that when you are one with Creation, what is yours to do, to be, and to have occurs and becomes an embodied Creation.

RECURSIONS: CI, CII, CIII, & CC

CI, CII, CIII, & CC [see Template] are each referred to as a *recursion*. You write three craving (CI, CII, CIII) recursions that are the same. In the beginning, using the <u>same craving</u> (A1) each time, supports the creation process while you are anchoring yourself in creating. So if you are Craving love [A1] in CI recursion, then you will write Craving love [A1] in CII and CIII recursions.

When manifestation begins to occur sustainably, then doing different cravings (A1 for CI recursion, A2 for CII recursion, & A3 for CIII recursion) is recommended.

The last recursion is called the *completion recursion* (CC). In this recursion, you take X1, X2, X3, which you will find at the end of recursions CI, CII, CIII after the word *embodies*.

Do not forget the completion recursion [CC], completing X1, X2, X3 with [XX]!

You as the Observer

The Miracle of Your Non-Physical Formlessness

In the preceding section, The Miracle of Your Physical Form, we looked at the flesh and matter design of a human being from a physical language perspective. Physical language is stimulus and response in association with craving. When what is stimulated responds, something comes into form. Craving stimulates creating. Creation responds. If what is being created can sustain and maintain its existence for a required period of time, such as an embryo, what is being created can embody. To embody is to become a self-sustaining, self-maintaining form.

In this section we will examine the spirit and energy design of a human being from both a non-physical and language perspective. This generates the second aspect of the Creation Exercises: the Observing.

The non-physical design of a human being is not formed by cause and effect. The non-physical simply is. Your non-physical being carries no emotions, no health or disease, no opinion, and responds only as part of a greater whole, whether you call that wholeness, God, Allah, Source, Creation, etc., is up to you. Your non-physical being is what you are after you die. Where your non-physical being connects into the Earth is through mind, chakras, quantum fields, matrixes, states of being, etc.

The energetic substance and intelligence of Creation in the physical plane is called consciousness. We are consciousness. There is no need for consciousness beyond the physical. Yet, in the physical, we are part of the substance and intelligence of Creation enveloping, surrounding, and penetrating everything that exists. We are where Creation reflects upon itself, gaining knowledge and recognition of itself through the multi-intelligent, multi-sensory, multi-dimensional system of the physical plane often referred to as a human being.

We are formed from the ineffable, the unexplainable, and the mystery . . . the playground of the non-physical side of our nature. We have become impoverished spirits, limited to finding a way out of suffering, an escape from our mortal existence. None of this gives us access to who we are as a spirit embodied into flesh. We have been denied the spirit treasure of being here.

Before you do the second half of the Creation Exercise, Observing, let's explore this realm of the formless, spirit, energy, being, the non-physical.

The hardest point to wrap your head around is that the realm of the formless is invisible and that we can only get somewhat aware of the ineffable nature of Creation by where the formless affects form. We cannot truly manifest anything into form that is meant to stay in existence, if we are not in alignment with the greater unfolding of Creation. We have no true manifestation if what is brought into existence carries no spirit. You see this in new cars, people's big houses, shopping malls.

> Without our spirit active in our flesh there can be no
> intimacy, ecstasy, passion or peace.

There is no problem that the beginning discovery of your design is stimulated by the need to escape suffering or confusion, but have you ever asked yourself what is beyond suffering and confusion? That is the intent of this work, to discover what life is like when the spirit and the flesh are one.

Spirit came into flesh to contain, unfold, and manifest its inherent qualities in the playing field of the physical. In other words, the Spirit had to bring its energy partially into matter to enjoy the delights of physical form. I am using metaphor here because we have no way to comprehend the true nature of Spirit. Spirit is beyond comprehension. And yet, my experience is that my Spirit delights in containing, unfolding and manifesting itself in the delight of being physical. What we call duality is simply where spirit and flesh dance together. Duality is not separation. Duality is a state of twoness in the oneness of Creation. Everything is part of an always and forever energy field, known as Creation. Physical form requires duality to exist. It is only when we forget that twoness is in oneness that we experience separation. The Creation Exercises are based in our dual nature of craver and observer. The metastate that occurs we have no language for. Imagine that the '/' in the following is what occurs when the twoness restores the oneness of its design: spirit/flesh, matter/ energy, physical/non-physical, infinite/finite, biochemical/alchemical, mortal/immortal, heaven/Earth, Cosmos/primal, human/being.

This is the phenomenon that occurs when doing both parts of the Creation Exercises: the Craving and the Observing. You move out of either/or, good/bad, right/wrong into another playing field. Rumi says, "Go to the field beyond all right or wrong doing. I will meet you there."

At this time most of humanity is adapted to separation and has little to no way to truly register unity. The challenge before us is to break the hold of separation on our design and open up into the mystery of what we are. It is not just a step by step process of recovering from suffering. It is in the magic of being alive, vibrant with creating, mastering observing, that we experience the awesome state of life when we are whole.

While we cannot see or even be fully present to Spirit, Energy, the Formless, etc, we can get present to the systems in our physical form that receive the information necessary to be embodied as spirit and flesh.

The first power of spirit is bringing the formless into form. The original Aramaic text of the Old Testament in the book of Genesis reads, "When in the beginning God created the heavens and the Earth, the Earth was untamed and shapeless."

The relationship between the formless and form, simply said, is the relationship between chaos and organization. Again in very simple terms, Creation is untamed and shapeless unless something brings order and shape to it. The Language of Creation brings chaos into order and the formless into form.

Having looked at matter, now let's look at energy.

Energy

Energy that comes from the Cosmos into the Earth is called Shakti in the Hindu tradition. Shakti comes from a Sanskrit word meaning to be able. Shakti is the sacred force or ableness that comes from the Cosmos, a dynamic force of Creation that shapes the entire Universe. While our bodies, especially in the West, are not yet able to hold the Shakti pouring into our Earth from the Cosmos, the Shakti will continue to pour in until our flesh and our spirit restore their oneness, their unified alignment with the rest of Creation. While our nervous systems shake as this energy pours in, the deep encodings within us are awakening. We have entered a time where energy and matter are preparing to dance the union of Earth and Heaven as we move in the conscious interactive relatedness of our flesh and our spirit.

Let's look at two of the Energy Systems within our physical form that move without deviation with Creation: the Solar Chakra and the Third Eye in association with the Mind of Creation

The Solar Chakra

Chakras are energy centers that carry spiritual power in the body. The energy system and spirit vibration of the solar chakra is called Manipura in Sanskrit. This chakra is considered the center of dynamism, a philosophical system that explains the Universe in terms of energy or force. The quantum field of Creation, moving through the solar plexus vigorously and progressively, is designed to be dynamic and certain in attitude. This is your seat of willpower and achievement and radiates life force energy throughout the entire human body. The solar chakra is associated with the power of fire and digestion. The solar chakra, is considered the "the center of etheric-psychic intuition: a vague or non-specific, sensual sense of knowing; a vague sense of size, shape, and intent of being".[10] The solar chakra draws its power from the sun.

The personality that develops during puberty is housed in this chakra, otherwise known as the *ego*. Those experiencing dysfunction of this chakra have difficulty obtaining or maintaining their personal power and suffer from a lack of self-esteem. Strong self-esteem is required for

---

[10] Llewellyn Worldwide Encyclopedia: *Manipura – The Power Chakra.* (n.d.). Retrieved from http://www.llewellyn.com/encyclopedia/article/254

developing intuitive skills. The solar plexus chakra allows one to really know oneself, etherically and emotionally. This intuitive chakra is where we get our gut instincts which signal us to do or not to do something.

The solar plexus chakra, associated with the fire element, can provide warmth and comfort or fear and terror. This chakra spans a wide emotional area. Some signs that the solar plexus chakra is out of balance are:

- Difficulty concentrating
- Poor ability to make decisions or judge a situation accurately
- Trouble taking action or getting things done

Some believe that by meditating on the solar chakra you can attain the power to create, destroy, or save the world.

The quantum field of Creation stimulates our nervous system awake and the energy of Creation begins to move through us. As the nervous system receives the download, the solar plexus chakra stimulates our solar plexus. We know this because this is where we have powerful gut instincts, a strong will, a clarity to act without understanding.

Without our original connection restored, our nervous system and our solar plexus react. Fight or flight, screw it or kill it, as well as anxiety and depression are some of the basic reactions to the miscommunication between these points of unity, these metapoints of our spirit and flesh.

The Third Eye & The Mind

The third eye in spiritual traditions, such as Hinduism, refers to the Ajna or brow chakra and is located between the eyes, slightly above the upper end of the nose in the brow. The third eye is a gateway into higher states of consciousness that exist beyond the Earth plane.

Human beings are designed to receive the messages from the Mind of Being . . . the Mind of Creation that formed humanity. The Beingness of the Non-Physical Self is not the same as the Beingness of the Physical Self and yet it is all Being. The Non-Physical Self concerns itself with the activities of the Universe and the Physical Self concerns itself with the activities of the Earth. The Non-Physical aspect of our being is designed to observe the physical plane being '*in the world but not of it*'. Our human-self comes from the Earth and our being-self comes from the Universe. Human beings are the metapoint, a connecting point of the Earth and the Universe, the spirit and the flesh, energy and matter, etc . . . . a METAself.

The Third Eye is often referred to as a *meta*-organ, gathering information from the greater whole of which human beings are a part. The third eye goes beyond the sensory system to gather information from the quantum energy fields of the Universe and bring it back into the human sensory system. When the energy/matter system of a human being is working in alignment with as above, so below the actualizing of greater forms for reality is effortless.

In our modern world, the denial of the esoteric and mystical as tangible aspects of Creation has left human beings bored, neurotic, and dysfunctional. When the innate function of the spirit/flesh system is distorted or broken, confusion and eventually insanity follow. For most human beings, the third eye is shut because the sensory system of what organizes thought cannot keep up with the extraordinary energy that comes with the awareness of broader aspects of Being. When a human being has the non-physical realm of the third eye receiving the messages from the Mind of Creation, the nervous system, the solar plexus, and the brain align properly. A capacity to perceive and actualize the magnificent experience of life every human being is designed to have is then actualized. Human beings are designed to perceive clearly and operate far more substantially then our present basis of thought allows.

Mystics, such as myself, have their third eye open and often people have trouble comprehending what we say. We are more in the Spirit relationship to the Flesh than the Flesh relationship to its Spirit.

In the power of the mystical or non-physical realm, we move as a being. 'Being' is hard to comprehend in our everyday world and yet is comprehensible in the mystical. In that the physical system calms and in the 'peace that passeth understanding' dynamics of existence become available that are not available when we are landlocked in our Earthly humanity.

Just as cravings dictate physical activity, the non-physical plane operates without any physical activity. The non-physical plane is dictated by witnessing or observing.

The third eye is the eye of the Observer, the truth teller, the way shower. The Observer is what looks through your earthly eyes when you can exist beyond earthly measures.

The Observer

The Observer is the consciousness of Creation.

Through the Observer we are present to the consciousness of a non-physical mind. The observer unfolds within us, opening us up into the subtle ways of Creation through our Third Eye. Through the observer we become part of consciousness itself. We bring the un-manifest formlessness of Creation into form on Earth. There is power in our direct connection to Creation. Without that connection we wind down, run out of steam, and give up. Connected to a non-physical mind that goes beyond physical form we have endless energy, are endlessly able to create, and stay present to what Creation is calling for as well as knowing what we are, as our unique and essential aspect of Creation.

Through modern quantum physics, we understand more of how Creation works. We have learned that the more we can become present to the living field of Creation and open up into it, the more we influence, in unity with Creation, what comes into reality. We are only now opening up into knowing we are a fundamental part of Creation and that we have say over how reality exists. We are just coming out of a perception of reality shaped by Newton's ideas that we have fixed properties and are part of the mechanical Universe that operates in a precision explainable way. We are seeing the cost of perceiving a reality where, according to Descartes, we are only our minds and our bodies are inanimate matter with no influence over reality, separated from

Creation. Our reality has become organized to protect and defend, honor survival of the fittest, and most of all win regardless of the cost. We are digging out of a reality that, in its unsustainable design, has left us lonely, isolated, afraid, and without vision. Vision is the gift of the Observer.

As we wake up into unity, our thoughts no longer fit in the system of reality we were born into. Our feelings break up the mechanistic hold on our thinking. We are confronted with being awake and alive, discovering the fundamental truth of our own being. What are we really and how are we really designed to exist? What is a reality consistent with our true state of being?

Without our ability to observe without bias, what we are feeling, thinking, experiencing, the Observer cannot bring into wholeness manifestation on the physical plane. That is why working with the Observing part of the Creation Exercise, until you can embrace the Observer aspect of yourself, is essential.

The Observing Templates are the second part of the Creation Exercises. We have become consumed by craving and yet we cannot manifest what we crave unless it is in alignment with our spirit. We are each a unique and essential aspect of Creation designed to manifest what is ours to do, to be, and to have. Our systems are restless for the state of stillness and silence that is the state of the Observer. Give the Observing quality time. You will be amazed how, through oneness with Creation, self-trust, self-awareness, and self-actualization can be realized.

Through doing the Craving AND the Observing Templates, the Creation Exercises create a field within which Spirit can come into Flesh, Energy into Matter, through what you crave whether a job, a relationship, or well-being. However without our complete design active, we may get what we crave but we will not be fulfilled by it. There is no fulfillment when the spirit of our matter is absent from what we create.

> "A quiet mind is all you need. All else will happen rightly, once your mind is quiet. As the sun on rising makes the world active, so does self-awareness affect changes in the

mind. In the light of calm and steady self-awareness, inner energies wake up and work miracles without any effort on your part."

Consciousness and the Absolute, Nisargadatta Maharaj[11]

Let's begin to study the Observing Template.

---

[11]   Maharaj, N., & Dunn, J. (editor). (1980). *Consciousness and the Absolute.* Brunswick East, Australia: Acorn Press.

TEMPLATE 1 OBSERVING

This is done after you have completed TEMPLATE 1 CRAVING. You need to have it with you to do this Template 1 Observing.

Before beginning to read the guidelines on the next page, please write out this Template on lined paper. (You can also download the Templates from iuwcinstitute.com/tmps in a print-friendly format.) A Creation Exercise has two parts: the Craving and the Observing.

DO NOT WRITE ON THIS TEMPLATE. When doing the Templates you must write out each word on a separate piece of paper.

OI: Read C1 and ask yourself: what have I observed in the time since I did the C1 recursion?

Observing _____ has me be present to $\boxed{P1}$.
Being present to $\boxed{P1}$ has opened me up into $\boxed{I1}$ (whatever in this moment you are opened up into).
Opened up into $\boxed{I1}$ has me have $\boxed{O1}$ (what you experience having).

OII: Read CII and ask yourself: what have I observed in the time since I did the C2 recursion?

Observing _____ has me be present to $\boxed{P2}$.
Being present to $\boxed{P2}$ has opened me up into $\boxed{I2}$ (whatever in this moment you are opened up into).
Opened up into $\boxed{I2}$ has me have $\boxed{O2}$ (what you experience having).

OIII: Read CIII and ask yourself: what have I observed in the time since I did the C3 recursion?

Observing _____ has me be present to $\boxed{P3}$.
Being present to $\boxed{P3}$ has opened me up into $\boxed{I3}$ (whatever in this moment you are opened up into).
Opened up into $\boxed{I3}$ has me have $\boxed{O3}$ (what you experience having).

OO:

Having O1 has me have O2.
Having O2 has me have O3.
Having O3 has me have OO (something you have not written before).

TEMPLATE 1 OBSERVING GUIDELINES

IN THE OBSERVING TEMPLATES YOU SIMPLY
STATE WHAT YOU ARE EXPERIENCING.

Tell the truth, whether what you are experiencing is pleasant or unpleasant, comfortable or uncomfortable, or devoid of any feeling whatsoever. Whatever is up is what there is to observe. Not what you *want* to observe or think you *should* observe. Simply write what you are experiencing . . . plain and simple. Don't edit, judge, doubt . . . just write whatever is there.

WHATEVER YOU EXPERIENCE IS THE TRUTH IN
THE MOMENT, THAT TRUTH WILL QUIET YOUR
MIND AND SET YOU FREE!

In the more modern societies, the suppression of emotion is immense. We are bothered by our feelings, whether they are pleasant or unpleasant. We ask, "What does this mean?"

Since feelings are not meant to mean anything, we end up in our heads! Our minds loop and loop and loop around asking, "What does this mean?" Other such frenetic confusions of thought shut us away from what there is to simply be present to.

Please do not search for meaning or analyze what comes up when you listen. I did a craving once, something like this: Craving peace of mind creates silence in my head. Creating silence in my head sustains and maintains balance. Sustaining and maintaining balance embodies joy.

When I look to see what came to mind since I wrote the craving what came to mind was: Observing I went to get my nails done . . . .

The observing exercise when done right literally exercises your mind until you can observe without reaction, without analysis, or limitation.

In the higher mind, the observer aspect of mind, you are simply present to what there is to be present to. In the act of being present, something opens up, and you have a new state of experience. You experience a resonance, not an explanation.

THE OBSERVING EXERCISES CAN BE BOTH PLEASANT AND UNPLEASANT.

While in the Craving you are declaring what you want your craving to create and it needs to be what you truly want it to be. Pleasant, resonant, etc. In the Observing that is not necessary. You need to know what you are present to. How else can you know what is going on? There is a powerful opening into a higher mindfulness hidden in your feelings and your experiences. When you get present to it, you open up into what is really there. Go for it!

FILL OUT EVERY WORD OR PHRASE EXACTLY AS YOU WROTE IT BEFORE.

It is important to fill out every word because you are changing the neural-synapses of your brain. By writing every word and phrase exactly as you carry it forward, you are reinforcing a new sequencing of thought patterning in your brain matter.

CORRECT Example:
Observing <u>I cried at the movies</u> has me be present to **bubbling joy**.
Being present to **bubbling joy** has opened me up into . . . .

READ RECURSION CI COMPLETELY AND THEN DO OI.

AFTER YOU HAVE COMPLETED CI/OI THEN READ CII AND DO OII.

THEN READ CIII AND DO OIII. DO NOT DO CC.

Recursions are the first three 3-sentence writing exercises. The letter and number of each recursion is highlighted in bold on your Template so you can identify them. (**CI**/OI), (**CII**/OII), (**CIII**/OIII)

SEE WHAT COMES TO MIND.

Step 1: Read the entire three sentences of the first Craving recursion: **CI.**

Listen to what comes to mind. This is essential. You are working with the wiring in the neural-synapses of your brain. Try not to think. Relax in a metastate of as little thinking as possible and listen until something comes to mind.

The unlimited potential of all Creation does not occur in logical thought! The unlimited potential of all Creation comes in abstract thought or in abstractions. In the Portuguese language, in The Aurélio's Dictionary, abstract is what expresses a quality or a characteristic separated from the object to which it belongs or is linked to.

YOU WANT TO OBSERVE RATHER THAN LOOK
FOR SOMETHING LOGICAL AFTER READING
THE CRAVING RECURSION

Pause as soon as you have finished reading the three sentences of each Craving recursion (CI, CII, CIII).

See what comes to mind.
It does not matter how random or seemingly disconnected your words are.

Example: You have read the first recursion of the Craving aspect of your Creation Exercise.

CI:
    Craving **love** creates <u>happiness</u>.
    Creating <u>happiness</u> sustains and maintains <u>well-being</u>.
    Sustaining and maintaining <u>well-being</u> embodies **relief**.

Then you get ready to write your Observing.

Stop! Pause! Listen!
What is there, regarding your life since you wrote the Craving aspect of the Creation Exercise that comes to mind reading the **CI**: craving recursion?

Example:
OI: Observing <u>I cried at the movies</u> . . . . Abstract! Might not seem associated but is what comes to mind.

NOTE:
You do *not* need to use only one word in the exercises.
Only one word is filled in to simplify the examples.

Do not use the words in the Craving aspect of your Creation Exercise in your Observing aspect of your Creation Exercise. Examine the following examples until you get a sense of it.

DO NOT write:
Observing **<u>love</u>** has me be present to . . .
or
Observing **<u>relief</u>** . . . .

DO THE FIRST THREE RECURSIONS FOLLOWING THE TEMPLATE DIRECTIONS.

DO NOT DO AN OBSERVING FOR THE COMPLETION RECURSION: <u>CC</u>.

Write out the first three recursions just as you have seen in the examples above (CI, CII, CIII).

Remember CI is a recursion with 3 sentences. CII is a recursion with 3 sentences. CIII is a recursion with 3 sentences. CC is a recursion with 3 sentences.

You do *not* do the Observing the same with (OO), the final observing recursion.

Now you have written Observing I cried at the movies . . .

WHAT ARE YOU NOW PRESENT TO?

The Observing Template brings you into a state of 'Be Here Now'. So, as you write what you observe, notice what you are present to in the moment of writing.

Example:
Observing <u>I cried at the movies</u> has me be present to <u>I feel more deeply now</u>.

Now you have written Observing <u>I cried at the movies</u> has me be present to <u>I feel more deeply now</u>.

WHAT HAVE YOU OPENED UP INTO?

When you write what you are present to, you automatically open up into new thought. Doing the Observing aspect of the Creation Exercise is like opening up a door with a rusty hinge. You literally get to where your neural-synapses aren't working. The purpose of the Observing Templates, of which there are two, is to open those neural-synapses up again. It isn't that you don't have a word. It is that you have limited thought capacity.

Be present to what you have written, and *see* what opens up. Then, let the thoughts rise. Write *those* thoughts.

Example:

Observing <u>I cried at the movies</u> has me be present to <u>I feel more deeply now</u>.
Being present to <u>I feel more deeply now</u> has opened me up into <u>fear of being too exposed</u>.

Now write:

Opened up into <u>fear of being too exposed</u> has me have . . . .

What is there?

Right there?

This is what you now have. This is called awareness.

Example:

Observing <u>I cried at the movies</u> has me be present to <u>I feel more deeply now</u>.

Being present to <u>I feel more deeply now</u> has opened me up into <u>fear of being too exposed</u>.

Opened up into <u>fear of being too exposed</u> has me have <u>caution</u>.

In the reality of separation, fear of being too exposed may occur as not good, bad, but in the reality of unity, you are simply observing what is present, opening up into that and seeing what is there . . . what you have. Having caution is a different reality from I am cautious. In the Gaelic language they would say, "I have caution upon me." A simple shift in a thought pattern like 'I have caution upon me' begins to create a different relationship to reality.

Having is the key to the kingdom, but you might not really get the full higher mindfulness of *having* until you have moved through more of the observing exercises.

Presently, we *try to have*. Having still shocks our systems. And yet, having is fundamental to the true nature of a human being. We are designed to have freedom, have love, have success, and have profound experiences. Remember what it is like when you first are attracted to someone. Remember the fear. This is the fear rooted in our cellular memory that fears having. Why would we fear having? We fear having because we remember having what we felt was ours taken away. Loss is a terrible master when that loss cannot be moved through. The trauma stays in our cells. We lost our connection to ourselves and each other as a species a long time ago. It will take something to reawaken those neural-synapses that carry our connection to Creation and give us access to having.

We were designed to HAVE! The Observing Exercise shifts us into the reality of having.

THE FINAL COMPLETION RECURSION IS DIFFERENT IN THE OBSERVING EXERCISE. IT IS NOT THE SAME AS THE CRAVING EXERCISE.

The fourth, completion recursion of the Observing Template takes the words in (O1, O2, O3) and fills in the blank on the sentences.

Having **O1** has me have **O2**.
Having **O2** has me have **O3.**
Having **O3** has me have **OO**.

OO is what you write that's new . . . what you haven't written before that builds the reality of having.

A Sample Creation Exercise.

CI: Craving a slimmer body creates having fun getting smaller. Creating having fun getting smaller sustains and maintains enjoyable healthy eating. Sustaining and maintaining enjoyable healthy eating embodies my precious spirit has her right home.

CII: Craving a slimmer body creates taking time for more of me. Creating taking time for more of me sustains and maintains my deeper being. Sustaining and maintaining my deeper being embodies longevity.

CIII: Craving a slimmer body creates having my life line up. Creating having my life line up sustains and maintains vitality. Sustaining and maintaining vitality embodies more fun things to do and be.

CC: Craving my precious spirit has her right home creates longevity. Creating longevity sustains and maintains more fun things to do and be. Sustaining and maintaining more fun things to do and be embodies vital shifts in my reality that serves what it is to truly be here.

OI: Observing that I haven't lost weight but I am feeling better has me be present to shifting into my way of eating is first and weight loss second. Being present to shifting into my way of eating is first and weight loss second has opened me up into I am moving into something permanent about my eating that is great. Opened up into I am moving into something permanent about my eating that is great has me have eating and supplements keep me awake to me.

OII: Observing sitting out under the stars at five am truly serves me has me be present to my love of silence. Being present to my love of silence has opened me up into understanding why eating has been easier lately. Opened up into understanding why eating has been easier lately has me have peace that my internal needs are changing.

OIII: Observing that some days I am still drained has me be present to a deeper underpinning of health is rising. Being present to a deeper underpinning of health is rising has opened me up into trusting the time it will take for this to all sort out. Opened up into trusting the time it will take for this to all sort out has me have a deeper stability in the face of change.

OO: Having eating and supplements keep me awake to me has me have peace that my internal needs are changing. Having peace that my internal needs are changing has me have a deeper stability in the face of change. Having a deeper stability in the face of change has me have certainty, not confusion.

The Being of a Human Being

Being is a state of existence within which you are simply being. In other words, to feel happy is different than being happiness. In Template 2 of the Creation Exercises, what we are as a Being is expanded on. For now, discovering and anchoring a state of experience you want to feel as a sustainable part of you, is enough.

TEMPLATE 2 CRAVING BEING

Before beginning to read the guidelines on the following page, please write out the Template on lined paper. (You can also download the Templates from <u>iuwcinstitute.com/tmps</u> in a print-friendly format.) Use this to guide you in doing Template 2 Craving Being.

It is best to practice first long hand and then use a computer but if you find writing tedious, using a computer is satisfactory.

This CRAVING BEING Template is also a primer, like practicing scales, to persistently increase your capacity to be.

DO NOT WRITE ON THIS TEMPLATE. When doing the Templates you must write out each word.

This CRAVING BEING Template focuses on what you truly crave being. Cravings A1, A2, A3 can be all the same or all different.

CI:
Craving being $A1$ creates being $B1$.
Creating being $B1$ sustains and maintains being $C1$.
Sustaining and maintaining being $C1$ embodies being $X1$.

CII:
Craving being $A1\ or\ A2$ creates being $B2$.
Creating being $B2$ sustains and maintains being $C2$.
Sustaining and maintaining being $C2$ embodies being $X2$.

CIII:
Craving being $A1\ or\ A3$ creates being $B3$.
Creating being $B3$ sustains and maintains being $C3$.
Sustaining and maintaining being $C3$ embodies being $X3$.

CC:
Craving being $X1$ creates being $X2$.
Creating being $X2$ sustains and maintains being $X3$.
Sustaining and maintaining being $X3$ embodies being XX.

TEMPLATE 2 CRAVING BEING GUIDELINES

This Template 2 CRAVING BEING is designed to generate a state of experience that is fulfilling. It is not what happens to us in life; it is how we *be* with what happens that is the source of a fulfilled life. In the Craving Being Template, you crave what you want to *be*.

COMPLETING THE TEMPLATE

CRAVING BEING is written out exactly the same way the Template 1 CRAVING is written out. The only exception is to remember to *include* the word **being** where it is written in the Template.

COMPLETE THIS TEMPLATE 2 CRAVING BEING CREATION EXERCISE USING TEMPLATE 2 OBSERVING BEING.

AN EXAMPLE OF CRAVING BEING CREATION EXERCISE

CI: Craving being in love creates being ready. Craving being ready sustains and maintains being available. Sustaining and maintaining being available embodies being excited.

CII: Craving being in love creates being aligned with opportunity. Creating being aligned with opportunity sustains and maintains being found by the man I love. Sustaining and maintaining being found by the man I love embodies being one with another for real.

CIII: Craving being in love creates being in a relationship that serves me. Creating being in a relationship that serves me sustains and maintains being with a man who fits my world. Sustaining and maintaining being with a man who fits my world embodies being fulfilled in relationship for the rest of my days.

CC: Craving being excited creates being one with another for real. Creating being one with another for real sustains and maintains being fulfilled in relationship for the rest of my days. Sustaining and maintaining being fulfilled in relationship for the rest of my days embodies being complete with life.

TEMPLATE 2 OBSERVING BEING

Please be sure you have completed Template 2 CRAVING BEING and have it available for reference in completing this Template.

DO NOT WRITE ON THIS TEMPLATE. When doing the Templates you must write out each word. (You can also download the Templates from iuwcinstitute.com/tmps in a print-friendly format.)

OI: Read CI and ask yourself: what have I observed 'being' in the time since I did the C1 recursion?

Observing being _____ has me be present to being $\boxed{\text{P1}}$.
Being present to being $\boxed{\text{P1}}$ has opened me up into being $\boxed{\text{I1}}$ (whatever in this moment you are opened up into being).
Opened up into being $\boxed{\text{I1}}$ has me be $\boxed{\text{O1}}$ OR
has me have a beingness* of $\boxed{\text{OO1}}$ [what you experience yourself being newly].

OII: Read CII and ask yourself: what have I observed 'being' in the time since I did the C2 recursion?

Observing being _____ has me be present to being $\boxed{\text{P2}}$.
Being present to being $\boxed{\text{P2}}$ has opened me up into being $\boxed{\text{I2}}$ (whatever in this moment you are opened up into being).
Opened up into being $\boxed{\text{I2}}$ has me be $\boxed{\text{O2}}$ OR
has me have a beingness* of $\boxed{\text{OO2}}$ [what you experience yourself being newly].

OIII: Read CIII and ask yourself: what have I observed 'being' in the time since I did the C3 recursion?

Observing being _____ has me be present to being $\boxed{\text{P3}}$.
Being present to being $\boxed{\text{P3}}$ has opened me up into being $\boxed{\text{I3}}$ (whatever in this moment you are opened up into being).
Opened up into being $\boxed{\text{I3}}$ has me be $\boxed{\text{O3}}$ OR
has, me have a beingness* of $\boxed{\text{OO3}}$ [what you experience yourself being newly].

65

OO:
_____

Being OI has me be O2. Being O2 has me be O3. Being O3 has me be OO (something you have not written before).

OO*:
_____

Having a(n) OO1 beingness has me have a(n) OO2 beingness.
Having a(n) OO2 beingness has me have a(n) OO3 beingness.
Having a(n) OO3 beingness has me have a(n) OOO beingness.

AN EXAMPLE OF OBSERVING BEING ON CRAVING BEING CREATION EXERCISE

CI: Craving being in love creates being ready. Craving being ready sustains and maintains being available. Sustaining and maintaining being available embodies being excited.

CII: Craving being in love creates being aligned with opportunity. Creating being aligned with opportunity sustains and maintains being found by the man I love. Sustaining and maintaining being found by the man I love embodies being one with another for real.

CIII: Craving being in love creates being in a relationship that serves me. Creating being in a relationship that serves me sustains and maintains being with a man who fits my world. Sustaining and maintaining being with a man who fits my world embodies being fulfilled in relationship for the rest of my days.

CC: Craving being excited creates being one with another for real. Creating being one with another for real sustains and maintains being fulfilled in relationship for the rest of my days. Sustaining and maintaining being fulfilled in relationship for the rest of my days embodies being complete with life.

OI: Observing being nervous about meeting anyone again has me be present to being shy. Being present to being shy has opened me up into being curious about what might happen. Opened up into being curious about what might happen has me be a bit fluttery in my heart.

OII: Observing being clearer has me be present to being more aligned now. Being present to being more aligned now has opened me up into being happy about relationship. Opened up into being happy about relationship has me be curious.

OIII: Observing being able for deep love has me be present to being ready to manifest someone with depth and truth as their nature. Being present to being ready to manifest someone with depth and truth as their nature has opened me up into being with someone who is their Original Design. Opened up into being with someone who is their Original Design has me be excited.

OO: Being a bit fluttery in my heart has me be curious. Being curious has me be excited. Being excited has me be open to a new future for me.

TEMPLATE 2 OBSERVING BEING GUIDELINES

Template 2 OBSERVING BEING is probably the most difficult to do. There is a problem with the way present language is constructed. Literally the way we create a sentence traps us in a limited thinking system. To get out of it we have to go outside established grammatical designs. This is especially true with this Observing. Remember to restore your neural-synapses we cannot stay in the same structure of language you were born into.

The intent of this Observing is to observe how you are being. You do it the same way you do Template 1 OBSERVING until the completion recursion when you have two options. You can also take grammatical license and mix and match.

Let's review the OBSERVING BEING Template.

SIMPLY SAY WHAT YOU ARE EXPERIENCING
YOURSELF BEING IN THE MOMENT

Tell the truth, whether what you are experiencing being is pleasant or unpleasant, being comfortable or uncomfortable, or being devoid of any feeling whatsoever. Whatever you experience yourself being is what there is to observe. Not what you *want* to be or think you *should* be or how you think you *should feel*. Simply write what you are experiencing being, plain and simple. Don't edit, judge, doubt. Write whatever is there.

WHATEVER YOU EXPERIENCE BEING IS THE
TRUTH IN THE MOMENT. THAT TRUTH WILL
SET YOU FREE!

Example:

CI:
> Craving being <u>healthy</u> creates being <u>alive with possibility</u>.
> Creating being <u>alive with possibility</u> sustains and maintains being <u>whole</u>.
> Sustaining and maintaining being <u>whole</u> embodies being <u>aligned with my body's highest good</u>.

OI:

> Observing being <u>afraid I will stay ill</u> has me be present to being <u>alert</u>.
> Being present to being <u>alert</u> has opened me up into being <u>reliable to get the help I need</u>.
> Opened up into being <u>reliable to get the help I need</u> has me be <u>at peace</u>.

DO NOT USE THE WORDS YOU USED IN THE CRAVING BEING TEMPLATE WHEN WRITING THE OBSERVING BEING TEMPLATE.

NOTICE THE END OF TEMPLATE 2 OBSERVING BEING IS NOT THE SAME AS TEMPLATE 1 OBSERVING.

THE OBSERVING EXERCISES CAN BE BOTH PLEASANT AND UNPLEASANT.

While in the Craving Being Creation Exercise, you declare what you crave being and what that beingness will create. You need to truly crave what you crave being, such as pleasant, resonant, happy, etc. (IF YOU ARE CRAVING IT, YOU ARE NOT ABLE TO BE IT YET).

In the Observing Being Creation Exercise, that is not necessary. You need to know what you are present to being such as being glad, being sad, being afraid. How else can you know what you are being?

FILL OUT EVERY WORD OR PHRASE EXACTLY AS YOU WROTE IT BEFORE.

It is important to fill out every word because you are changing the neural-synapses of your brain. By writing every word and phrase exactly as you carry it forward, you are reinforcing a new sequencing of thought patterning in your brain matter.

READ EACH RECURSION OF TEMPLATE 2 CRAVING BEING JUST AS YOU DID IN TEMPLATE 1 CRAVING.

(**CI**/OI), (**CII**/OII), (**CIII**/OIII)

SEE WHAT COMES TO MIND

Step 1: Read the entire three sentences of the Craving Being recursion.

Pause as soon as you have finished reading the three sentences of each Craving Being recursion (CI, CII, CIII). Read the three sentences of one Craving recursion at a time followed by one Observing Being recursion.

CI:
>   Craving being <u>in love</u> creates being <u>fulfilled</u>.
>   Creating being <u>in love</u> sustains and maintains being <u>happy</u>.
>   Sustaining and maintaining being <u>happy</u> embodies being <u>in partnership</u>.

>   Then you get ready to write your Observing Being.

DO THE FIRST THREE RECURSIONS FOLLOWING THE TEMPLATE DIRECTIONS.

DO NOT DO AN OBSERVING ON THE FOURTH RECURSION: <u>CC</u>.

WHAT ARE YOU NOW PRESENT TO BEING?

The Observing Being Template brings you into a state of 'Be Here Now'. So, as you write what you observe, notice what you are present to being in the moment of writing.

Example:
Observing being <u>sad</u> has me be present to being <u>needy</u>.

Now you have written Observing being <u>sad</u> has me be present to being <u>needy</u>.

WHAT HAVE YOU OPENED UP INTO BEING?

When you write what you are present to *being*, you automatically open up into a new sense of being or something being available that wasn't before. Doing the Observing Being aspect of the Creation Exercise is like opening up a door with a rusty hinge. You literally get to where your neural-synapses aren't working.

Be present to what you have written, and see what opens up. Then, let the thoughts rise. Write *those* thoughts.

Example:
Observing being sad has me be present to being needy.
Being present to being needy has opened me up into being insecure.

Now write:

Opened me up into being insecure has me be in need of help.

What is there?

Right there?

This is what you now have. This is called *awareness*.

We have little or no ability to *be,* particularly in the western world. Being what we have been taught to be is acceptable. This exercise taps the language of your Being, creating a path toward wholeness.

In Template 1 Observing, you are working on having. In Template 2 Observing Being you are working on being.

> **Without *being* we have no stamina for life, for change,
> for risk. In this Observing Being exercise you are
> maturing your being.**

THE FINAL COMPLETION RECURSION IS DIFFERENT IN THE OBSERVING BEING EXERCISE.

IT IS NOT THE SAME AS THE CRAVING OR CRAVING BEING TEMPLATE OR IN THE OBSERVING TEMPLATE.

Being **O1** has me be **O2**.
Being **O2** has me be **O3**.
Being **O3** has me be **OO**.

Example:
O1:

Observing being <u>ready</u> has me present to being <u>okay with the way things are right now</u>.

Being present to being <u>okay with the way things are right now</u> has opened me up into being <u>excited</u>.

Opened up into being <u>excited</u> has me be **open to what's next**.

OO:

Being **open to what is next** has me be **O2**.
Being **O2** has me be **O3**.
Being **O3** has me be **OO**.

OR:

OO*:

Having a(n) **OO1** beingness has me have a(n) **OO2** beingness.
Having a(n) **OO2** beingness has me have a(n) **OO3** beingness.
Having a(n) **OO3** beingness has me have a(n) **OOO** beingness.

4

Restoring your Connection to Creation

A young woman with a broad rimmed garden hat, a peasant blouse, and baggy linen pants walks down the street. She is smiling. Then a tear slips down her face as a radiance feeds the air around her. She is clear and is moving with every step in what is heis to do, to be, to have.

A young man, well put together in blue jeans and a Sunday shirt, stops her. "Are you okay?" he asks. She laughs, "Yes!"

She looks into his eyes, "What do you crave?" she asks.

He blushes, "Oh I don't crave anything!" thinking she misunderstood his intentions.

She laughed, "No, I didn't mean that. What do you crave to be for you, crave to do for you, crave to have for you?"

His upbringing had taught him well, "I don't crave anything just for me. That is selfish."

"No it's not. There will never be another you. You are unique and you are essential. That is why you were born," she responds settling onto a park bench motioning him to sit beside her.

"Now, what do you crave?"

He sits cautiously. The ripples of what separates him from his Original Design create a disturbance, but something else, something deeper, beckons.

"Name one thing you really crave to be, or to do, or to have," she says, smiling that radiance that drew him to her to begin with.

"I crave happiness," he admits, feeling awkward using the word crave.

"Why? What would happiness create in your life?"

"I don't know," he said startled. He had never thought about why what he wanted was important nor what he wanted it to create.

"That's okay. You see something happened to our thinking. We were born into thinking about things. Thinking about things does not let us create with our thoughts. We just think and think about being happy but we don't have any access to being happy. Do you see that?"

"Yes! Wow!" he gasped. A welling up of sadness caught in his throat and he said, "Ohhhhhhhh . . ."

Calmly she says, "Not to worry. We have another thinking within us that is more of who we are and gives us access to creating what we crave in our lives."

"What is that thinking?" he says, puzzled.

"I call it the Language of Creation. You see, we are made up of the same substances of the earth and the cosmos. If you look at everything around you, the trees, the birds, the sky, you could say they are all having a conversation with each other. The language they are all engaging in is the Language of Creation. They are craving and creating all of the time together. What if something happened and they forgot what created them and how to interact with what created them?

"Jeez," he said. "That would be awful."

"Don't you feel awful sometimes because you can't figure out how to get what you so deeply want? What you crave?"

"Yes." The air stood still. The birds stopped singing. The world was silent.

As she began to speak, the radiance returned.

"Those feelings are there because you were born into a reality where everyone forgot what created them and that they are a part of that. I call what created you Creation."

He looked up and smiled. Something had stirred past the disturbance . . . a connection to something that had been lost. "I crave happiness and what I crave happiness to create is a world I want to be part of."

Delighted she clapped her hands and almost hugged him. "Great! See what dominates the world you were born into is separation. Everything is separated from everything else. Without connection nothing can last—not relationships, not governments, not even food supply or jobs. Everyone begins to protect themselves from each other, defend themselves from being harmed, and fight or run in fear because they can no longer connect with anyone, even themselves."

"What do we do about that?" he asked.

"Well, doing hasn't done very much, wouldn't you say?"

He nodded.

"What if there isn't anything to do and there is something to be?"

"Huh?"

Delighted he had paid attention for so long, she jumped into an outburst of sentences, "You see something is happening! Maybe it just couldn't happen before now. Your Original Design is connected to everything. Your design is part of the great design of Creation. AND it is waking up . . . coming back online. That design is your being. See every one of us is a unique and essential design of Creation.

Pausing to take a breath, she continued, "What if you are miserable because you are trying to wake up and come online as what you came to be and you just don't know how to get there??"

He burst out laughing, thinking to himself, "She is nuts."

But . . .

He didn't stop listening.

"You see," she continued, "if you could live as the language of your Original Design, just like the trees and the birds, you would not feel separated from anything.

Plowing on, she continued, "Okay! See, you have to know what you want, what you crave to create, to have it come into existence. BUT! Even if what you crave comes into existence, it has to stay in existence. To stay in existence, it has to sustain and maintain itself. Like the sun. The moon sustains and maintains itself. You don't have to put it in the sky every evening. Your heart beats without you having to start it every morning. SO! What would sustain and maintain a world you want to be part of?

"Whack job or miracle?" he wondered.

Before he could question what she said, he blurted out, "love".

The air around him quickened. Something woke up in him saying that word that went past the word itself.

"Maybe I am being the Language of Creation?" he thought.

"Okay!" she said starting into another torrent of words, "Now let's look at what happens when something can sustain and maintain itself. It embodies!" Sweeping her arms up into a grand gesture, she looked at him only to be met by deer in headlights eyes.

She reached out and took his hand and looked gently into his eyes. "We all came here to embody."

"What is she talking about?" he squirmed as he felt her hand pulsing with excitement.

"Didn't your dad's sperm crave your mom's egg and together they created an embryo that had to sustain and maintain itself at least five months before it had everything it needed to embody as you?"

Aghast at her example, he could not miss her point.

Holding his hand firmly and looking into his eyes, she said, "So what would sustaining and maintaining love embody?

A fierce fight started in his logic but he just kept asking "What would sustaining and maintaining love embody?" noticing he felt like his entire life was on the line. Then he felt as if his brain let go, and his mind exploded. "Sustaining and maintaining love embodies bliss."

He just sat there. Everything felt different. The world was bigger. There was suddenly more room for him.

He teared up and turned away.

She sat very still. Absorbing the sunlight and slipping off her sandals feeling the soft grass under her toes, she knew there was nothing to do. He had touched the true design of himself. "There is no sunset, no success, no amount of money that compares to that," she sighed wistfully thinking how few people ever got to know what they actually are. "Ahhhh, but the magic of it all when they do."

"What is this?" He whispered. Afraid the moment would go away and he would forget. Never to feel that again did not feel so good.

"That is your being," she whispered back. "You see you don't have to look outside of yourself to find what you are. You already are what you are. You just didn't have access to it. You are trying to get back to you. Otherwise there would be no logical explanation for everything you have gone through to get better, to find yourself, to feel whole."

"What is my being?"

"Your being is the 'you' that never got separated from your Original Design. A long time ago something happened way before we were born that separated us as a species from our Original Design. We no longer felt a part of what created us. We thought we belonged to our family, our tribe, our country. But our original belonging was with Creation. We belong to what made us. Our Original Design of Creation is what we are made of, what we're part of, with the innate attributes and skills and gifts of Creation itself."

"What happened?"

"You get access to what you are when you are in direct connection with Creation. You are a container of Creation. Not the limited container of the world you were born into. You were born into a container that limited or denied your ability to get access to the container that is yourself. Not only are you more than you think you are, you are capable of becoming more and more and more of what you are. Your real container is your being where you become more and more *self* aware and *self* contained. You begin to be able to experience yourself beyond your present limitations. You begin to experience you as the next greater aspect of Creation that you are becoming. You return to being a metaself who lives in greater and greater comprehension of what you came here to be, do or have."

She let go of his hand, straightened her sunhat and put her sandals back on her feet.

"Would you like to meet me here tomorrow? We could see what you observe over these next twenty-four hours."

"I would really like that," he said with a sincerity he had not felt for a long time.

He woke up the next morning noticing that something was different, but he wasn't sure what. Life didn't feel so confusing somehow.

She was sitting on the bench waiting for him. She hugged him and asked, "What have you noticed since we met yesterday?"

He thought and said, "I noticed I don't feel so confused."

"Okay," she said, "now you have come this far, let's go a little further. Ready?"

"Yes," he said, "Let's go," and smiled.

"Imagine that Creation is a great big never ending field, an unending container within which everything that is lives. In quantum physics, you would say a quantum field. But for us, let's call it a living field. You are part of that living field so you are a field within a field. Wild, huh?!"

"I'm listening," he said, knowing there was more.

"Well, imagine that Creation is watching you and you are watching Creation. In ancient times being the observer or the watcher, was considered a very high state of being. Ready?"

"Ready."

"Let's say that craving, creating, sustaining and maintaining, and embodying are part of the physical laws including our flesh and that observing is part of non-physical laws, of spirit. We don't speak the language of spirit or the cosmos anymore. In our separation we got so lost in doing, we forgot the power of being." She sighed, lost for a moment in the loss of spirit in these times.

"And?" he said, interrupting her thoughts.

"You are both spirit and flesh, physical and nonphysical. So you need to remember that the non-physical language of spirit is different than the physical language of our flesh. Once upon a time there was no separation between the non-physical and the physical. Language carried the energy of spirit and the matter of flesh. This is the Language of Creation. A language that returns you to who you are as flesh and spirit, carries the design of your true nature, your wholeness."

"What is the language of spirit, of the non-physical?"

"Remember a non-physical language is non-physical so it is different than physical language. Where we crave in the physical, we observe in the non-physical. The language of flesh lives in time. The language of spirit lives in the moment. Close your eyes for a moment. It is easier to walk you through it than explain it."

His eyes closed, she asks, "So now, remember observing you were not so confused. Go back to that moment, okay?"

"Okey dokey," he smiled.

"What are you present to?" she asked.

"When I observe I am not so confused, I am present to being calmer."

"Now stay in the moment, being calmer. What does that calm open you up into?"

He could feel it . . . the field of Creation. He could feel himself being present to being confused. Somehow 'in the field' being present to being confused wasn't so confusing. Instead there was a calmness he hadn't experienced before and that calm was like a door that opened him up beyond where he had been. He let her words guide him as he moved in this beautiful state of being. "What does that calm open you up into?"

"When I felt that calmness, I did what you said and I opened up into joy."

"Now be in that joy like a place in the field and see what you have there."

"I have more room to be me."

"This is the place of spirit. In spirit, you could also be present to sadness. In spirit, there is no judgment. There is just what you are present to and what that opens you up into. Open, you get to see what you have that you can't see you have, when you are observing your life."

He felt like he had experienced himself in a way that was more familiar to him than in all the time he had been alive. And yet, he knew that he hadn't experienced himself for such a long time that he would have to live in this language for awhile to get himself all the way back.

He looked over at her and she had a booklet in her hands. "These are the exercises that give you access to what you are as part of Creation . . . what you are actually designed to be, how you uniquely think, and what you came to create as an essential part of existence here."

She stood and gave him her hand. "Walk with Me."

As they moved through the park, she began to speak, "You have touched your being now. You will begin to discover and be able to hold the larger nature of yourself. As you unfold into your design, you will uncover innate skills and capacities that were just not available in a broken and fragmented reality you've had to exist in. You've been in a broken container. Without including what you are, you are like shattered glass. You can see many reflections of yourself but you can't see yourself. Through doing these Creation Exercises in this book, the craving and observing, your container will more and more include all that you are. Then you begin to experience what was essential about you being here and you will be able to be it."

"Why didn't I meet you before now?" he asked, the green of the trees was greener. He loved the sound of the children's voices where two days before he had found them irritating.

"I don't think we could have met before now. Humanity has gone through many cycles. Many centuries have passed as we have worked to recover what we are; this last century being psychological. Before the psychological era, it was totally permissible whatever a parent did to a child, or whatever a man did to a woman, or whatever a country did to a tribe. There was no thought that it was wrong or unjust. But as we moved through the spiritual era of Buddha and Christ and Muhammad, we began to see that there was something wrong with not remembering that we were love and that we could love our neighbors as ourselves and turn the other cheek. While we are still wrestling with the obsessive attention to violent thoughts and violent actions, many of us feel there is another way to exist. While we are still awakening from the trauma-based realities that we have grown accustomed to, we are in the beginning of a new reality of discovery. No longer hidden or lost, new and ancient knowledge is uncovering the truth of what we are. So our post 2012 era is answering questions we didn't even know how to ask: "What is a human being? What are you? What created you here? What is your design? What are your innate skills and capacities? More and more evidence shows we are matter and energy, spirit and flesh, organized by the physical and non-physical, the biological and the alchemical. Jesus Christ said he was born of his father in heaven. He showed he was born of spirit and had all the attributes of spirit but came in flesh. Our flesh and our spirit have for centuries been separated from each other. We have been enculturated to believe that our flesh is evil, and that our spirit is not attainable here on earth. That enculturation exists at a cellular level. Until recently we ate whatever we wanted and flagellated our flesh, only beginning to be aware that traumatizing our bodies, we are damaging our body's ability to be one with our spirit.

During the psychological and industrial era, we became so mental. Everything became analyzed, dissected, and categorized. We lost touch with the power of higher spiritual experience reducing God to a solution that hopefully would get us out of the mess we were in.

Underneath the trauma of being separated from what we are and the traumatic conditions that rose from that separation is the memory of what we are when trauma is no longer organizing our lives. The ancient Language of Creation has never died and is rising in our cells. This simple language awakens and you discover you as the Language of Creation. You are designed by its principles, by its laws, by its structures, by what lets things come into existence as whole, as a whole operating system without any separation from its Original Design. The Language of Creation is you and your thought plane is designed to operate in that language. Your languaging is unique to you, not someone else's languaging, yours. And in your languaging, you discover your truth. There is not one truth. There are many truths.

Your truth begins to get revealed as you do the exercises and that truth begins to manifest. You will delight in discovering the beauty of your design and finding yourself doing what you came to do, being what you came to be and having what you came to have. So much more than you could ever imagine. You will know what none of us know and what none of the rest of us has access to. You will have experiences that none of the rest of us have. You are an expression of Creation in the flesh and in the spirit. It's worth the journey."

The day was ending. They both knew it was time for them to part. He squeezed her hand with one hand and the book with another. "I will never forget you," he said.

She laughed and spun around, "More importantly, you will now never forget you."

5

Language of Creation II

Creating Reality

[an excerpt]

He smiled humming as he noticed how light-footed he was coming down the path to meet her. He had dressed in a stylish boyish outfit. Reflecting on the past year, he thought about how much fun it had been to become what he was today. He loved what he wore now, when before, he had not thought much about it. He had not found the job he wanted but in the job he presently had, he could say easily what was his to do and not do, so the job was more satisfying. He hadn't found the one he wanted to stay with for a lifetime either, but he was not tormented by finding her, because he knew through his connection with Creation that finding her was his to do when it was time to do it. Amazingly other people could even hear what he said even when they didn't understand him.

He laughed.

He knew that every day he was more and more his connection with Creation. He could not explain the shift that had occurred. Problems were no longer a source of suffering. They were what he used to do the exercises on, that she had given him, and were now safely tucked in a small brown book in his pocket. When he finished doing the exercise on the problem, he could see how the problem wasn't what there was to pay attention to, but that the problem was connected to some deep connection to life that he had. Then, almost like magic, he found he was anchored in his deep connection to life that made the problem and everything get sorted out like an adventure not a dilemma.

Returning laughter pealed out of the hazy day and he looked up. "You did it!" she squealed. 'You restored your connection to Creation! Look at you. You are your unique and essential self!"

"And more and more every day!"

He hugged her unwilling to let her go. They just stood there entwined as, now, he burst out everything that had happened since they had met. "I belong! I belong to myself! I still don't feel like I belong in the world the way I want to . . . . (smiling) crave . . . yet, but not belonging the way I want to doesn't make me feel separate anymore. AND I can find my place of connection at work, when I date, even when I buy stuff. I am connected. Before you and the exercises, that just wasn't true!

She untangled herself from his enthusiastic arms, smoothed her long basic black skirt and her hair, and pulled him down beside her. "Until you are connected to yourself, you cannot be connected to the world."

"Well," she said as if speaking to herself, "that isn't quite true."

Looking at him with her impish eyes, she said, "What if I told you that there is no world except the one you are connected to? That everything you see that you think is the world may not be the world where you can do, be, and have what is yours to do, be, and have? What if I told you you don't have the world you belong to because you haven't created it yet?"

"You mean it is not my fault that I don't feel like I belong to the world in a lot of ways? Are you saying that there are other worlds?"

"Yes!" she said clapping her hands, "Many worlds exist in the same place at the same time. You perceive what everyone else says is so in the beginning. I call that the 'Great God They Said So'! You take for granted it is real but don't you feel like there is something else to see and to know that is missing in the world around you? That something you feel is the access to creating a world that is yours. The world around you begins to be where you can be what you came to be, do what you came to do, and have what you came to have. It is a brain thing. Your brain became hardwired to a certain perception of reality when you were born. But if your brain had been functioning properly, you would have been born into manifesting the Template of reality that is yours to be a part of. Your world where you belong."

He didn't question what she said. He just knew like the last year, that until he was in the mind of what she was saying, he could not know what she was saying.

"So how do I do that?"

She slid a small purple book out of the large pocket of her white quilted jacket and handed it to him.

"Another exercise?" he asked grinning.

"Yes," she nodded. "Now you have restored your connection to Creation, get ready to create your world!"

Epilogue

The Language of Creation is You as the Reality of the Future

There comes a moment in history when how we understood ourselves ceases to be accurate. In that moment, our mind reaches into the greater intelligence of Creation through our DNA and begins to align with what is now occurring. We are life. We forgot but that does not change that we are life. We are life lifing. Like all life, our DNA, the Template of our existence, shifts to stay part of the greater existence that we are a part of.

I, as a mystic, a seer, and a prophetess, have been tracking the human mind since I got here. And at the same time tracking shifts in reality. That is what I am designed to do. I learned that shifts in reality activate deep encodings within our DNA that awaken our cells and eventually our minds to the actuality of what is occurring. As the template of our existence awakens, how we think stops at the edge of a new horizon. In ancient times when our connection to Creation was intact, we listened and could align. As we lost that connection, we lost the power of our minds as part of the wonder of Creation.

These Templates, of which you learned two Cravings and two Observings, are designed from the human being's innate connection to Creation. Because you can only comprehend reality to a limited degree and cannot yet comprehend how reality will be shaped now in alignment with the shifts in Creation, the Creation Exercises keep your brain/mind/spirit/flesh exercised so as the shifts occur you can shift also and keep realigning until the new futures forming are actualized.

If you choose to be a student of your own consciousness and wish to take the journey of your own expanding beingness, then you might want to take the entire journey. This book addresses and activates these DNA encodings that are now rising and realigns your mind to be part of Creation.

This is the language of Level One.

As you experience the phenomenon of being part of Creation more and more, you will come to the edge of your consciousness and you will need to expand your awareness to the next level. Your next level of expansion is creating the world that you belong to. Yep, that is right. Once you are reconnected to your unique and essential aspect of Creation, you can create the world you are part of . . . a place you can do what you came to do, be what you came to be, and have what you came to have. Level Two brings you into the mind of the Creator who craves what reality is for him or her. There are two Cravings and the same Observings as in Level One.

Then there is a final level, Level Three. We have not visited this realm of Creation since we were indigenous to this planet and to the cosmos. In Level Three, your mind is part of Creation itself. You build structures through language where complex organizations of existence can occur. An example would be where work, money, and self expression come together in unity with one another and you getting to be in the reality within which that occurs. This is the first Creation Exercise of Level Three. The second Creation Exercise of Level Three is where you no longer crave. You observe. Your observing influences reality and reality begins to shape to the greater awareness of life that you are. The last Creation Exercise is the Template of Embodiment. This is where you awaken through language your spirit in your flesh. This is the great I AM . . . the embodied spirit in human form . . . a living field of Creation that generates reality for all life. This is our future calling. This is the dream of Creation that we are becoming a part of.

I have worked as a mystic and a seer for almost a half a century. Now, at this age, the things that I foresaw and even had trouble believing so long ago, are now an active part of our life. I have tracked your consciousness, your unfolding through the lives of thousands of people. There is no question that your internal turmoil and/or envisioning are the substance of a future now rising. You are its seed. When you do the Creation Exercises, you are a Creator rediscovering your role in Creation. Your life cannot go forward in its glory and its substance without feeding the larger budding future that is now coming online.

If your interest is being all you can be this lifetime and being active in what you are as a Creator with Creation, then this is a lifelong study beginning here that can manifest unbelievable results.

Namaste!

Tantra Maat

APPENDIX

Testimonials

"How many systems and exercises have I learned since 1979 when I started my search into the deeper realms of me wanting to know who am I, what is my purpose and what am I here to do? They are way beyond my memory at this point, but I am deeply grateful and appreciative for the stepping stones they have each been in my self discovery. For me the Creation Exercises hit the jack pot! I remember, years ago, the very first time I listened to Tantra teach this written exercise, called the Creation Exercises in the Language of Creation course, to a group of us that Marilyn and I had gathered in our living room. She was whizzing through her passionate delivery, in a state of such exuberance that I felt completely lost as I was trying to grasp writing out something I craved. How could this very simple question, about what am I craving, stop me so suddenly in my tracks and hook me simultaneously with a dogged determination to 'get it'. I believe I was beginning to experience that there was something here to warrant my staying present to this wild delivery of flying words, and scribbles on a large pad and easel up in front of the room as my feelings of complete intimidation and school memories of 'not getting it' were drowning me in feeling stupid. Through my held back tears, I could feel that in this seemingly simple exercise of 'craving . . . . creates', something very profound was happening here. Little did I know, the exercise/tool/gift that I was being given would replace all the many exercises I had learned over decades of dutiful learning. The simplicity of 'what do I crave like the seedling, pushing through the asphalt, craves the sun', I loved. That image always moved me from my exterior wonderings right into unraveling places and knowings, deeper and deeper within me that I hadn't felt before or known how to access. Then, getting that the I, my SELF and I, that I opened up into, in these exercises, is me . . . . creating, really knocked my socks off! From the truest place of Self as a creator, within the Unity of all, THIS is the ride I wanted and I'm a ridin!

I have watched these Creation Exercises become my anchor, my bridge, my direct line to the 'all that I am' AS the creator that I AM. I turn to these Creation Exercises whenever I have a predicament that keeps bothering me, I need a breakthrough to a deeper knowing of what is going on, and most especially to create! From the truest place of my SELF, owning who I AM, hearing the call of what is mine to do, to be and to have, there is only to create from now on.

Out of complete love and support for myself I found myself setting up a 'station' in the corner of our living room that looks out on to a beautiful view of the foothills of the High Sierras. It is a little table and chair with a very old laptop computer that is happy in its elderhood to hold only my creation exercise writings. It is always there, whenever I am ready, to listen and write. To this day I continue to be stunned when I go to my corner and write ;-)

Thank God this book is finally being written, so the gift and power of this work is available now, for anyone who hears or feels its call. Bottom Line, it is a transmission for our times that knows no bounds."

Georgia Dow
July 17, 2013

"The Templates I did in the Language of Creation courses were deeply impactful in a way that I have never experienced from any previous written exercises in other courses. The results were nothing short of revelatory to me. Even though I found them challenging to do, the Template results were worth all my efforts. Now I can see that the Templates were intentionally and brilliantly designed to circumvent the rational 'trickster mind' and open up a much deeper level of awareness that has an integrity all its own, and as such, it is far more trustworthy about truth-telling. Since I was no longer able to deceive myself, I discovered clarity of truth that allowed me to take responsibility for inner conflicts in which I have felt stuck for a long time. When the 'lights went on', I experienced a new kind of mental freedom which even years of psychotherapy had not given me. The Templates are a tool that penetrates to a place of inner truth that comes from the unconscious mind, a place I can trust completely."

Susanna Dimmitt
August 1, 2013

"[Doing the Craving Template] I could hardly choke out the words as they were laced with lifetimes of profound emotion and tears. They seemed to be escaping from deep within where I had kept them, locked behind closed doors. A teacher of higher truths? My life's purpose? Divine? Essential to the Unified Field? A high vibrational Being? I was a blubbering mess after the 4th recursion, ending with: "Sustaining and maintaining what my SELF is for me is grace personified embodies what my SELF is for me is God, the I AM presence."

Still makes me cry.

This was an authentic experience of the TRUTH of that remembrance. I am in Awe. I am in profound gratitude for Tantra for birthing the Language of Creation process. It is genius. While my head sort of 'knew' who I was, I never was really able to let it in. Really let it in. NOW I remember.

So I let it in."

Maggie Crane
August 5th, 2013

"When I write the Templates, a door opens, and all that I love enters in to greet me, and guide me. As well, the power lines of the universal matrix come online, strengthening their energy, sending out more offshoots of the grid to tighten the weave of universal support. Templates, no matter if they are personal, or geared toward the whole, are crucial to the strength and intertwining of community. How do I keep this knowing in my cells so that it will remind me of doing them daily, if not for the joy of simply connecting? It is as though, when I write them, I have this love fest with my universal elders, angels, and team. They are present, holding me, loving and respecting me. What pure bliss to have this open door of connection available to me every day if I so choose?"

Liz Geyer
August 28th 2013

"The impact of doing the Creation Exercises for me is two-fold. First, it keeps me operating with the Power of Energy that far surpasses any 'energy level' I might be able to generate on my own. Second, it builds a living field in which new paradigms might occur that allow me to shift. I may live with my problems and complaints for a while, but when that living field—the next level of consciousness from which those problems and complaints are meant to get solved and dissolved—gets strong and builds momentum, the a-ha moments are undeniable and utterly irrevocable.

Let's face it: Maybe it's true, there is always somethin'! And, let's also be honest: There is neither magic pill to 'fix it', whatever 'it' is, nor is there escape from the constant challenge of the natural phenomenon of expansion and contraction. Yet, there will also always be the constant calling to rise to the occasion and the sheer need to move with the opportunity provided by obstacles. The Creation Exercises help me to maintain a presence of mind to see those opportunities clearly and to see what might be occurring as obstacles instead as occasions to create! And, to do so from my authentic nature as well as my authentic relationship to Life, Creation, The Greater Living Whole itself."

Anonymous

Frequently Asked Questions

Answers compiled by staff of Tantra Maat Inc.

1. **What is the best way to practice the Creation Exercises?** The best way to practice the Creation Exercises or Templates is by following the guidelines given in this book step by step. Keep the book by your side for reference as you do your first few Templates as it takes a while to get into the rhythm of doing them. Handwrite the entire sentences, use resonant words/phrases in the blanks of the craving part, do not repeat words/phrases exactly but find ways to adjust how you phrase things. Perhaps writing in a quiet space, one you feel comfortable in, is optimal when writing the Templates, but not required. Most important of all is to just take your time with the Creation Exercises. Don't begin with having huge expectations of them. Just begin with the motivation that you are going to give them a go and see how they feel for you. That eases any expectation around getting them 'right', which of course is old programming. There is no getting them wrong, but you will see a progression in how and what you write, and more interestingly, *from where* you write over time.

2. **When is the best time to practice?** There is no best time, except what is resonant and life enhancing for each person. Using the Templates continues to open us up into dimensions of what it is to be human, which includes using resonance/life enhancement as a guide more than rules and shoulds.

3. **Should they be handwritten?** In the beginning, it's very important to handwrite them, until you become really familiar with how they all work and feel.

4. **What is a good way to organize them?** A 3-ring notebook.

5. **Can I ever write them on my computer?** Yes, but not in the beginning.

6. **How do I organize them on my computer?** Individual exercises can be separate documents, put into monthly files. Easiest is to organize them by date.

7. **Is writing the Templates like meditating?** This is a multidimensional response. Keep in mind there are many kinds of meditation. There is also a wide spectrum of how people understand, relate to and use meditation. All of the mindfulness practices I know of have a life-enhancing impact on a person's world. There is a constructive impact on the biochemistry. This means fight/flight is calmed or transmuted. The body's normal restorative abilities are freed up again (they get 'jammed' in stress, especially long term stress or traumatic experiences, and if jammed too long, dis-ease and disease begins to manifest). Mindfulness practices also free up a person's ability to think, especially in terms of executive function such as planning, making decisions, having the ability to be present to what is going on in one's environment that permits responding more than reacting. I would even venture to say that long-term, disciplined use of meditation has one be aware of and able to include/use their spectrum of intelligence, but that is not typical for people in modern western society, even if they are quite accomplished or spiritually developed. These are some significant ways that using the Templates is indeed a meditative practice. **What is the difference?** There are several significant differences in the Language of Creation Templates over other forms of meditation, at least with regard to most people of modern western civilization. Possibly the most significant difference is that using the Templates is designed to grant conscious awareness of one's own system. This means people a) remember they are, always have been and always will be a vital, integral aspect of the greater whole of which we are a part. This remembered or restored experience eventually becomes part of one's daily experience, daily reality. b) Becoming more consciously aware of one's system also means people remember they have a spectrum of intelligence as part of their very natures. For example, some are more sensory than others, some lead with their emotional intelligence, etc. We are not limited to the spectrum of intelligence called 'intellect' or 'cognition'. c) A really important aspect of gaining conscious awareness of one's own system is that a person gains the ability to have greater

ownership of and articulation for what they are present to. All of these things combined allow us to relax into a creation-based life.

8. **Will using the Templates help my meditation practice?** Using the Templates will enhance or empower your meditation practice, your prayer practice, or any other engagement with life that is important and authentic to you. Using the Templates does not replace anything, unless it is authentic for you to be finished with something. Using the Templates does not impose a belief system, or put pressure on anyone to engage with X instead of Y. Rather, using the Templates allows a person to become clearer about the elements of their world as choices.

9. **Should I meditate before or after doing the Templates?** Whatever is most life-enhancing for any given person is the best choice. No one needs to meditate to have the Templates be effective. However, doing the Templates can and often does trigger a contemplative, meditative state. So, if you find yourself in a meditative state after completing the Templates, there is no reason not to amplify and expand this state by sitting in meditation and stillness for a while after your practice.

10. **How often should I do them?** This depends on the person. When we teach the Templates, we use guidelines recommending each person do at least a couple a week, which means both the Craving part and the Observing part. I think it is optimal to write at least one Template per day, as part of your daily 'spiritual/emotional/mindful hygiene' and sustenance. Sometimes people feel the need/desire to write more than one per day. It is important to listen to this inner guidance. Again, trust your Self and you will know. Writing Templates daily allows for your life in a creation based paradigm to sustain, maintain and embody.

11. **How will I know when to move onto the next Template?** When using the same Template for awhile, if it is time to move to a different one, the one you've been using begins to feel 'flat', or as if you are not getting as much out of it. Then you will know it is time to progress to the next Template.

12. **What are the common pitfalls?** The most common pitfall is to stop writing the Template, or more accurately, not listening to your Self regarding when it is time to resume. People get to

a point where they feel good, feel solid, get some results, get opened up into new aspects of their authentic world and opened up into their creation based paradigm, then they slip into thinking using the Templates is just one more technique to do and they drift away from using them. Because the restoration process of the Language of Creation is real, and often due to the sheer grip and momentum of the conditioning of the system we were born into, people forget that using the Templates regularly is what supports being able to live in a creation based paradigm. Often they do not notice cues of their system prompting them to resume writing the Templates until something extremely challenging happens and they get reminded. The second pitfall is that people do not fully get the fact that these Templates are not affirmations for manifestation, which has also become conditioning over the last 60 years or so. People seem to have a hard time comprehending that affirmations are a much weaker, less effective approach than generating an environment within which what you crave occurs.

13. **Where do people normally get stuck?** There seem to be 4 general places people get stuck, all of which reflect how conditioned we are into the separation based paradigm. These are not in any special order, that is, the order I'm listing them does not mean anything. 1) Many times people have trouble with what 'craving' represents. They have been conditioned that wanting, desiring, and being of the material world is somehow less spiritual, makes them less good people, etc. So it is hard for some people to move with 'craving'. 2) Another way people get stuck is thinking the Templates are about fixing a problem, or are a way to try to manifest like with affirmations. 3) Many people have trouble accepting their own magnificence; possibly the single greatest stuck place is the thought form 'what is wrong with me?' Related to this is difficulty knowing how much Creation needs and wants them, how vital each person is to the whole of Creation. 4) And finally, many query themselves, wondering if they are doing the Templates 'right'.

14. **How do I know if I'm doing them right?** First, to keep training yourself into creation based language, discipline yourself to think and speak in terms of 'am I using the Templates correctly

or accurately' instead of 'right or wrong'. To say 'am I doing this right' automatically calls up 'what is wrong', puts you into an either/or position and a position to have to judge your performance rather than moving with what becomes available as you write the Template. Asking if you have written the Template correctly simply puts you in a space of technical correction if that is called for. This may sound like splitting hairs, but it is actually an important distinction. Language creates and perpetuates reality. Another way to know if you are writing or using the Templates correctly is to follow the instructions and pattern of the Template. That is an additional technical side of the matter. Experientially, you will know if you are using these correctly because you will have an experience of relief from fight/flight/stress along with an experience of sturdiness and peace that is not connected to circumstances, manifestation, etc. You will have accessed creation based biochemistry and your experience of your connection with the greater whole of which you are a part, allowing your spectrum of intelligence (which includes experience of connection to Creation) to flow.

15. **I have a lot of problems in my life, where is the best place to start with the Templates in relation to those problems?**
First it is really important to remember that using the Templates is not about fixing problems. Fixing problems is part of the separation based paradigm. The Templates promote each person's creation based existence of generating the environment within which what you crave can occur. Having said that, look if there are common threads to the problems (creation based language would be 'challenges' or 'limitations to my full Self expression' etc). If there are common threads to your challenges, or underlying themes, then use that to write your craving part of the Template. For example, I had several issues and limitations that ended up with common threads regarding health, vitality and being out of shape. So I started writing cravings using all sorts of variations as I kept becoming present to the various metapoints of these matters, over a period of about 3 years. Another way to use Templates to engage with your problems is to prioritize them and just start with one at a time.

16. I have great difficulty focusing, where should I begin? Because of the ways the Templates shift your neural synapses back to registering life/input in the spiral, inherent way our brains were meant to operate, just the use of the Templates should help with focus. So just start with the fundamental Template. Another way to begin would be to write a Template: Craving focus creates _____. Or Craving being more focused creates _____ (and of course write the associated observing part of the Template). Or write a Template regarding why you want to improve your ability to focus, or on craving the elements of life/environment that improve your focus (for example, Craving less distraction in my life creates _____). There are a lot of reasons for lack of focus, lots of ways this shows up, and lots of reasons why one wants to improve focus.

17. My mind is very busy, what would be a good craving to begin with? Again, the way your mind is busy, and/or why, factors in to providing the best response. So you could start with: Craving a calmer mind creates _____. Craving less to think about and juggle creates_____. And other permutations. Simply using the Templates will have a calming effect, since they shift you from fight/flight to a creation based biochemistry. Next, being moved into our other intelligences can have a calming effect, since the burden of information processing is no longer forced onto just one line of thought, so to speak (our intellect and cognition). Also, many times our minds are busy because we have been conditioned into the 'doingness' of life: how much can you get done in a day, with constant pressure to do more. Your success depends on getting results, yet certain kinds of results do not really count as successful in this day and age, such as being a stay-at-home Mom. We live in a culture that values and emphasizes the concrete, and has been called a 'fast food society'. Even though we have quotes like "stop and smell the roses", many sectors of society do not encourage or even actively discourage 'stopping to smell the roses' or other forms of just being. Add to that all the TV we watch until late at night, so many cities with lights and noise going all night, the ability to work until late at night with lights on, computers on, using video games, etc., it's no wonder our brains are overwhelmed and revved up.

Our body's biochemistry is revved up too, in response to this bombardment of relatively low-level, unremitting stressors. So of course a person could seem to 'be' a nervous person, or to have a busy mind, or have trouble focusing as indicators of attempts to recalibrate in the face of unhealthy aspects of modern life. Being stuck in the 'either/or' of this modern society, it is difficult to return to wholeness until something allows you to reconnect with, restore yourself to, your spectrum of intelligence; something that by its nature lets your system balance its biochemistry and become present to your authentic life design and what is yours to do/be/have (and thus what is not yours to do/be/have). All of this permits a true recalibration of your life, with a consistent ability to continue the design of your life as you gain capacity with knowing what is life enhancing for you and what is not.

18. **I'm a very nervous person, what would be a good craving to begin with?** I'd say start with the basic craving, the first Template, because 'nervousness' could also be called 'anxiety' or 'hypersensitivity' or 'highly strung'. Write a craving part of the Template like this: Craving being less nervous creates _____. Or, perhaps you are discovering that you are a very sensory sensitive and instinctual person, somewhat like a creature of the wild, like a deer. Often that does not fit well in modern society, especially if you live in a city with lots of noise, movement, lights all night, crowds, and possibly limited access to the quiet of nature or have a demanding corporate job. So, starting with the first Template will first help calm the fight/flight you may have been in a long time. Then it will begin to give you access to the range of your intelligence, including being able to value that you lead with sensory and instinctive intelligence. Then as you continue to learn to be present to what you are present to, and to trust your awareness/experience of what is life enhancing for you, you will begin to comprehend what supports your system, what life design is accurate for you, etc. All of this coming together will result in a natural reduction of 'nervousness' and a natural enhancement of the life-enhancing aspects of what has been reduced to 'you are nervous'.

19. **I find I'm not very grounded, what Creation Exercise could help me with this?** Craving being more grounded creates

_____ is one option. Also, "Observing I'm not very grounded has me be present to _____" and from here you may be able to determine what you would crave upon writing this observing. That is not part of the 'newbie' guidelines, not how we recommend people just learning do this unless this specifically comes up.

20. **I don't feel much in my body and find the Observing Template very difficult, what can I do to help that?** This is interesting, as many who feel out of body have more trouble with the craving part, which attends to the physical aspects of the system. Some people have written cravings such as Craving being more in my body creates _____. Observing the observing part of the practice is so hard for me has me be present to _____ (and other Templates around the different facets of this issue). Some people have found that writing the Observing part with another person helps (ie while they write their Templates). Others find being in an environment that is grounding, supportive and nurturing helps.

21. **Is using the Templates like a spiritual practice?** Yes and no. It is a spiritual practice in the sense of restoring you to your daily awareness of direct connection to Creation. This means you remember you are a vital aspect of creation, that you are needed and loved by Creation. By using the Templates, you will be restored to knowing yourself as a metapoint of energy and matter, spirit and flesh, divine and local selves. But I know that these aspects you get restored to are fundamental to existence, they are just how life is, like gravity is gravity. So in the sense that a spiritual practice represents, reinforces, upholds or grants access to a composition of traditions, beliefs and doctrines, no the Templates are not a spiritual practice.

22. **I journal a lot, is doing the Templates the same as journaling?** No. Free-form journaling, such as keeping a diary, is very likely to have you write from the very thought forms you are conditioned to by the system you have been born into, including being past-centric, maybe present-centric, but the focus is still inescapably 'what is wrong with me/life/others' and fixing a problem or processing. Some journaling practices are structured, and grant access to a specific quality, such as improving your

writing skills, for example. But even some writing practices I've seen in therapeutic environments are still based in fixing a problem, still based in fixing what is wrong with the individual; even if the author thinks they have avoided that, still operate in a separation/fear based reality. The Templates are the first structured writing practice I've encountered that is present and future-centric, which, by their very nature, moves people out of fight/flight, opens people up into the next greater whole of themselves and their world, and into all the creation based elements of life we have been discussing in the responses to other questions.

23. **Should I keep my completed exercises?** It is a good idea, because then you can look back over what was important to you over the time period you've saved completed Templates. More importantly, it becomes clear how your life has moved through various recursions of moving to the next greater whole. You will be able to tell all the subtle and overt dimensions of changes, results etc., that you have had, and often in non linear ways. You will see how you/your life has quantumed, how it has deconstructed/constructed, contracted/expanded, what has gone out of existence or come into existence, and what is your current next greater whole. This means you will experience being aligned with and part of Creation, in a living, life-enhancing way.

24. **Should I do the same craving Template at different times to see if anything has changed?** Well, since life is always deconstructing/constructing, contracting/expanding, moving to the next greater whole as some things go out of existence and others come into existence, even if you start with the exact same words, your craving of today will not be the same as the craving on that matter from a year ago, or even a month ago. So you will see what has changed. Again, it is not a matter of 'should', but is this life-enhancing?

25. **I've been doing the Templates a long time now and feel ready to move on—what do you recommend next?** First, remember this could be an indicator of the pitfall described earlier. The Templates are not about fixing things, but this is a very difficult idea to get past. Many people still think the Templates are useful mostly when things are 'going wrong'

(which means when manifestation is not happening or when they are feeling bad about themselves etc). The Templates are useful in times of "things going right" too, to continue to reinforce the creation based paradigm you have begun to inhabit. However, many people do arrive at a new level of their worlds by using the Templates, and they need to live or grow into those levels for awhile. At these points, some do not feel drawn to write Templates for a time. When that happens, I strongly recommend you set an appointment on your calendar for once a week, and write one Template regardless. Or, set an appointment for a few weeks out, even maybe a month, then on that day do at least one Template just to gauge your system. Then depending on the results, set another appointment to check back in. Remember, a few weeks, months, even a couple of years of using the Templates does not necessarily completely take the conditioning of the separation/fear based world out of your system. We have become the by-product of this system we were born into after eons even before this lifetime. Using the Templates is not a set of techniques to get better or fix problems or manifest like in affirmations (which is a way of fixing something). It is a practice that strengthens a paradigm, restores dimensions of being human that have been compromised over time. So if it is authentic that it is time to set the Templates aside for a time, set something up to remind you to resume them later, or just reduce the amount of times you write them to maybe once a week.

Contact Information

To download the templates in a printable format and to find
out more about working with the Creation Templates please visit
The Creation Institute at www.iuwcinstitute.com/tmps

We would love to hear your experience of using the
Creation Templates, please email locbook@tantramaat.com

For further information on the work of Tantra Maat,
you can go to her website at www.tantramaat.com

Tantra Maat Inc, Tantra's corporation, is committed to awakening our
Original Design and training and developing our innate talents and
gifts to be our unique and essential part of the future calling.

Printed in the United States
By Bookmasters